NORTHERN WARRIOR

Richy "Crazy Horse" Horsley

warcrypress.co.uk
Richy Horsley (c)

ISBN: 978-1-912543-01-4

Northern Warrior Produced by www.wacrypress.co.uk (part of Roobix Ltd: 7491233) on
behalf of Richy Horsley, Hartlepool. Copyright © Richy Horsley 2018. Richy Horsley has
asserted his right as the author of this work in accordance with the Copyright, Designs and
Patents Act 1988.

Cover Photos by Dean Kitching

Printed and bound in Great Britain by Clays, Elcograf S.p.A

Find out more at: facebook.com/CrazyHorseHorsley/

DEDICATIONS

For my dad Tommy and my mam Brenda who have long since departed this mortal coil, without you my story would have been so different. Thanks for everything and see you on the other side.

For my wife Wendy thanks for being by my side every step of the way.

FOREWORD

Richy Horsley, Husband, Father, Grandfather, Friend and Fighter

If you say the name Richy Horsley in the town of Hartlepool, most will say they know him or know of him, the latter would probably be the most accurate statement.

99% probably don't really know him, I'm proud to say I'm in the 1% that does.

For a man who has made such a mark in life he's a very private person, more happy at home reading a book or watching TV, a far cry from the Richy people perceive to know.

But people don't pick up a book to read about a normal caring member of society, they pick it up to read about the man Richy was, so on that note strap in and fasten your seat belts and enjoy this incredible journey.

Kevin 'Bulldog' Bennett
Former Commonwealth Lightweight Champion
Former World Lightweight Bare Knuckle Boxing Champion

Contents

INTRODUCTION

It was an unusually hot and humid night and the heat in the place was unbearable. The underworld faces had turned out to see the hard man from the North fighting one of their own, a cockney.

I was 39 years old and top of the bill at the Hammersmith Palais in the West End of London.

The two thousand strong crowd had a couple of hundred of my supporters in amongst it and they were all in good voice. They had travelled a long way and I wasn't going to let them down, I had to win.

The night was in full swing and fight after fight, the crowd roared their men on, eager for knock outs and claret, the more brutal the better. They were all there for the blood sacrifice. If you closed your eyes and listened to the crowd, you could be in the Rome Colosseum 2000 years ago. Nothing had changed we were the modern day Gladiators.

It takes a special breed of man to climb into the ring and fight in front of a crowd all baying for blood.

The dressing room was like a furnace and there was no air to breathe but finally after what seemed like an eternity, the lights died down and the Master Of Ceremonies announced my introduction. A big roar went up from my supporters and my entrance music came on and started booming out. It was my turn and time for action.

CHARLES BRONSON

I had been a part of the underbelly of the hard man scene for a long time and I was friends with the notorious prisoner the world knows as Charles Bronson. We had exchanged lots of letters and pleasantries over the years and had some laughs along the way.

Some of the things he'd say would be from a man who was a deep thinker, a man who knew what life was all about and had his fair share of experiences. In other words he didn't waffle on about bullshit and didn't suffer fools. I found him to be an intelligent bloke and not the monster he was made out to be. Whenever there was bad news, like bereavement in the family, he would send a lovely letter and a drawing, very thoughtful with kind words. After a few years I felt like I was getting to know him and I was put on his list of visitors but was refused to be allowed to visit him by the authorities for some unknown reason.

I was becoming popular around the country with the release of Julian Davies excellent book 'Streetfighters'. My mug was on the front cover and I had a 16 page story in there. Maybe that was the reason I was refused a visit to see Bronson.

Charlie loved painting and drawing and his art work was getting better, he loved his art. He was developing his own unique works of art, the 'Banksy' of the prison world, and some of his paintings sold for a small fortune. The good hearted Bronson would donate lots to charity.

One day I got a letter off him saying his art was going to be displayed and he was really pleased about it, what an achievement. I was to be guest of honour at the art display in Leeds and had to contact the organiser whose number Charlie had enclosed. I did consider it a privilege that he chose me to be his guest of honour out of all the people he knew. I was busy working and completely forgot that I had to phone the guy who was running the show.

My memory was refreshed when I got a letter from the organiser saying the show was coming up and would I phone him ASAP and he left his number. I can't remember what happened but I never phoned him and it slipped my mind. It was a big thing for Charlie and he was donating to charity out of the event. I didn't realise how much it meant to him until I got a letter through the door which had a few choice words for me, he wasn't happy at all. He wanted to know why I disrespected him by my no-show. Lots of other people turned out so what was my excuse. He said it was all for charity and I should be ashamed of myself. If I was in his shoes no doubt I would have felt the same.

My reaction to it was to write Bronson a strongly worded letter which I know would have had him fuming. It went something on the lines of – minus the swear words- 'Who do you think you are wanting me to be at your beck and call and drop whatever I'm doing to go to your art show. I'm nobody's fool so don't give it the big one to me',

'You think you are a top fighting man. Well come on and tell me who have you fought? Nobody who can fight that's for sure, all you've done is beat road-sweepers and bums in bars. I've fought trained fighters and I've fought at a much higher level than you. I'm a trained fighter and I'm leagues above you. You wouldn't last a single round with me before I knocked you spark out'. Anyway you get the drift of the letter.

A couple of weeks later I was contacted by a representative of Bronson who said Charlie was due for a parole hearing and it looked like he could be getting out.

3

"Charlie wants to fight you if he gets his parole and it could make you both a nice few quid" he said.

As the months wore on, the people involved behind the scenes had the wheels in motion. Bronson v Horsley was going to be held in a big marquee tent in London and everyone who was anyone would want to be there. It would be an event not to be missed, the rich and famous love things like this and the television and papers would lap it up. A notoriously famous inmate (Bronson) coming out of years in solitary confinement to fight unlicensed would be a huge spectacle. I was hoping and praying that Bronson would get parole.

He always kept himself in shape and once said:

"I'm the king of press-ups and sit-ups. I once did 25 press-ups with two men on my back, and I've squatted with three men on my shoulders. I've been making prison records for as long as I can remember. Show me a man half my age what can pick up a full sized snooker table. I can. Show me another man who can do 1,227 press-ups in an hour. I can. I once went eight years without using weights, then I went into a gym and bench pressed 300lb ten times. I'm 5ft 11in and weigh 220lb and I feel as strong as I did when I was 21. There's something deep inside me that pushes me on. I'm a solitary fitness survivor".

An unlicensed boxing promoter in London had asked me a few times to headline one of his shows but I always said no. Now with the Bronson fight looking like a real possibility I said yes. I wanted to shake a bit of ring rust off and sharpen my tools.

I took this serious so I got into full training, I done my roadwork three times a week and gym work Monday through Friday. It was a real hard slog and sometimes I felt like packing it in but I cracked on with it. I had some very hard spars and my sparring partners didn't give me any easy days, almost every session I had a bust nose and I hardly ever had nose bleeds in the past. I used three sparring partners and all of them were quality fighters. They were England number 2 amateur Middleweight Mark Denton, ABA Heavyweight Novice champion Paul Malcolm and Craig Denton who retired undefeated as a pro at 9-0. After eight torturous weeks of that I had lost two stone and felt brilliant. I wrote every training session down so when I looked at it I knew I'd put the work in and was ready.

I fought an experienced lad who had about 40 fights called Tony Louis who was around 17 stone, strong and tricky. The fight was originally scheduled for six rounds but the show went on too long so at the last minute they cut it to four rounds as I was the last fight of the night. I could hear my supporters singing "Horsley, Horsley".

I knew he was a spoiler who boxed on the back foot so I jumped on him because I didn't want him to get into any kind of rhythm. I cut the ring off and closed him down. I kidded a right hand and switched my weight over in a split second and BOOM, a crushing left hook thudded into Tony's ribs and he was on the canvas in pain. The ref counted to ten and I won by knockout to the delight of my travelling supporters. Tony Louis got two broken ribs. I've always had a good punch and as you get older the last thing you lose is your punch. Celebrity gangster Dave Courtney came up to me and said:

"Richy you can't half hit, I'm fuckin' glad you're not hitting me!"

The win over Louis was well received and everyone was talking about the upcoming Bronson fight. There was a lot of excitement and anticipation surrounding it and I told everyone that I'd knock

Bronson out. I couldn't see anything other than a win for me. Yes he was a strong as an ox, yes he was a street fighter, yes he was going to be very dangerous especially in the first round, yes he holds the world record for press ups and yes he can punch, yes, yes, yes. The difference was I was schooled and had fought at a much higher level. I could take a really good punch and I could fight under pressure and stay cool and focused. I knew all this and thought Bronson was underestimating me.

The news finally came that took the wind out of everyone's sails and the fight went out the window when Bronson was denied parole. I was devastated by the news but had to take it on the chin.

When I first wrote this book back in 2002 I'd just had a hernia op and was chilling out recovering when I put pen to paper and I only got a few copies printed. Charles Bronson wrote a nice tribute for me which I'll include here:

"Some men are just born to fight, it's in their blood. They can't do anything about it, they have to fight. A fighter isn't necessary a psycho or a thug, far from it. Most fighters are gentlemen, men of pride and men of honour. But if you fuck with a fighter you've got to expect the consequences. You are going to get hurt, you may even die. No man is invincible. Even the fighters at times feel defeat and some die, but bet your arse on it, if they don't die they are coming back for more. Richy Horsley is one of these special breed of men and I'm honoured to know the man" Charles Bronson

What a lovely tribute that was from Bronson, it makes you feel good when someone says something nice like that. A few years after our spat we became friends again. We are a lot older so there is no chance we would ever fight now. Our fighting days are behind us.

In 2008 a film of Bronson's life was made and the lead role was played by Tom Hardy who did a great job. A few years later when Charlie was allowed to view it he said it was 'Theatrical, creative and brilliant', he had nothing but praise for Tom Hardy and they became friends.

Charlie has since became a born again artist and in 2014 changed his name by deed poll to Charles Salvador, in tribute to the artist Salvador Dali. He is trying to get away from his violent past, he has served his time and learned from his mistakes and, I for one, think he should be given a chance to prove he is rehabilitated and be set free. He said "It's non-violent all the way. It's a peaceful journey from here on. My heart is at peace and my mind is set on art." Under his new name he has been creating works of art.

Charlie recently married Paula Williamson, who has appeared in Emmerdale and Coronation Street. "I'm madly in love with Charlie and he's madly in love with me and we just want to be a normal couple" said Paula.

I wish them the best of luck.

SLAYING THE DRAGON

I was brought up by Tom and Brenda Horsley, they were the only parents I knew and as far as I'm concerned are my 'real' parents. They had a baby what died at six months old and Mam couldn't have any more children, so when the opportunity arose to 'adopt' me, they did. They brought me up with a lot of love because I was wanted; there was no childhood abuse of any kind. We didn't have much regarding money but I never wanted for nothing. I always had clean clothes and a cooked meal and never went hungry. I loved my childhood and would go back to it in a heartbeat if I could.

When I was five years old my parents told me I was adopted, I loved The Lone Ranger back then, my mam said I just looked at her and said "Did I have my guns on".

Another story from when I was five was when I got drunk for the first time. It was New Year's Day and my parents were in the kitchen cooking the dinner and Mam's friend Ann was left with the instructions to 'keep an eye on him' because there in the corner of the room was a table full of drinks.

My mam's friend was feeling the worse for wear after seeing in the New Year until the early hours and was soon asleep on the couch. That's when I made my way over to the table and was looking at all the different coloured bottles. I was like a kid in a sweet shop, only they weren't shouting eat me they were shouting drink me! I poured a glass of sherry and had a mouthful mmm! This is not bad I'll have some more. Then I drank another glass. It didn't take long to start having an effect and I was rolling around on the floor laughing my head off, pissed as a fart as they say.

Ann woke up with the noise of me laughing and Mam came in the room and pointed at me but looked at Ann and said "What's the matter with him?"

It didn't take long to realise what had happened as the bottle of sherry had no lid on and had been guzzled. "I'm sorry I shouldn't have fallen asleep" Ann said. Too late now there was nothing they could do about it. Mam was worried sick and wanted to take me to the hospital but my dad was the calm one and said "Put him to bed and let him sleep it off", so I got carried upstairs to sleep the drink off at five years old!

Mam was beside herself with worry and was constantly checking on me in case I choked on vomit, which happens a lot, I know a few people who have died that way. Anyway after a good kip I went downstairs and stayed on the couch for the rest of the day nursing my first hangover. I remember my dad, who was always the joker, sat laughing at me. It brings a smile to my face when I think about it.

It wasn't too long after this episode that I had my first fight. I had been getting intimidated and bullied by an older kid from down the street and would often run in the house crying after being hit by him. Don't you just hate bullies, all bullies are cowards. I despise them. My parents would tell me to stop running in the house crying and start sticking up for myself.

It was a sunny day, I remember it like it was yesterday, and I spotted the bully around the corner. I decided it was now or never and plucked up the courage to shout him. As soon as he saw it was me his face changed to a growl and I called him a few names, which was like a red rag to a bull and he came charging after me.

My parents were out the front enjoying the sunshine when I bolted up out of breath with the bully in hot pursuit. When he saw my parents he stopped running and started walking towards me, our eyes locked and I knew then what I had to do. I don't know where I got the courage from, maybe because my mam and dad were watching it unfold and I didn't want to back down in front of my parents. It was fight or flight and I chose to fight. I walked towards him and when he was in striking distance I planted a big right hand on the side of his head and it hit him on the ear. I stood there with my fists clenched ready for more. I remember the pain on his face and the tears in his eyes as he walked away holding his ear. He was probably in shock as well and I couldn't believe what I'd just done, I had slain the dragon. He never bullied me again. My parents were over the moon and couldn't stop smiling.

A short time after this I was at my Grandfather's (Mam's dad) house fun fighting in the front garden with my older cousin Michael. I managed to get on top of him and pin him to the ground. Michael must have thought he was just going to throw me around but it didn't turn out that way and while I had him pinned down he said to me "Do you want a real fight?", whether he felt a little embarrassed by being shown up by his little cousin I don't know. I was trying to digest the words he just said to me when he repeated them, "Do you want a real fight?", I looked up and my dad was stood on the step and was watching the proceedings and laughing. Michael got his answer in a split second as I said 'Real Fight' and smashed left right combinations into his face. He usually suffered with nose bleeds but today's was a really bad one, there was claret everywhere. After I had been shouted at and told off I made eye contact with my dad and he was grinning like a Cheshire cat.

A few years after this, Michael had a fight with a boxer friend of mine called Tony. The fight was only seconds old when Michael's nose started cascading with the red stuff from Tony's jabs. Michael had no chance trying to box with Tony so he quickly tried another tactic and took Tony to the floor. While they were both on the deck, Michael started rubbing the blood from his nose into Tony's eyes and the fight got stopped. Both claimed victory but nobody actually won.

Another fun fight that turned serious was my first fight at school. All the lads were fun fighting at play time and one particular boy was stronger than everyone else in his gladiatorial play wrestling. When he came up against me we were both rolling around on the floor, each trying to get the upper hand. I could feel he was stronger and had steel determination but I wasn't going to back down either so, call it sixth sense or something else, but I knew it was about to turn serious and within a couple of seconds the first punches came. Instinct told me to get to my feet as I didn't want to be mauled by the stronger lad, so I jumped up and so did he. You know when you see someone who has murder in his eyes, well this lad had murder in his eyes and I've never forgot it even though it was so long ago. He came rushing at me and I hit him with a one two. My heart was beating through my chest and my legs were like jelly with the adrenaline because this was real life and I was in danger. He kept rushing me but as soon as he got close enough I'd hit him with a one two. A teacher ran over and broke it up, there was blood on my hands and my legs (Mam always had me in short trousers in those days) off his nose. I didn't have it all my own way as I got a black eye. Many years later I saw him in a pub and we shared a couple of pints together and talked about our fight when we were kids. It's nice to bump into old timers and reminisce.

That fight must have given me a bit of confidence because soon after, a girl called Tina who was a distant cousin, told me she was getting picked on by a certain lad and asked me if I would tell him to leave her alone. Why lads want to pick on lasses baffles me. She pointed him out to me and I went over and got hold of him by the scruff of the neck, pointed to Tina and said "You see that girl over there, she is my cousin so leave her alone from now on" and then gave him a taste of his own medicine with a few punches and kicks and he screamed like a girl. He never touched her again.

I was soon to be on the receiving end when I went into first year junior school, I think it's called year three these days. I got my dinner and sat down to eat it and a lad in fourth year - year six nowadays - started picking on me trying to look good in front of his pals. I was scared and didn't dare say anything to him and then he spat in my dinner. I kept quiet and never said anything to Mam and Dad when I got home. Things like this make you not want to go to school so you fake an injury or an illness, but the next day I went as normal. The same thing happened, the same lad started picking on me and the pig spat in my dinner again. He had no reason at all to pick on me it wasn't like I was a threat of any kind. That's two days in a row that I'd had no dinner and I wasn't going to eat it with spit in it. This time when I got home I told Mam and Dad and they were disgusted and wanted it nipping in the bud. My dad was old school so he went to see some friends who lived a few streets away, whose sons were in the same year as the bully, and told them what had been occurring. The next day I had to go and see one of the Collins brothers, they were expecting me, and I had to point out the bully. I found Michael Collins and told him who I was and he said 'show him to me'. I soon spotted him and said 'there he is' and then Collo got hold of him and pointed at me and said "Stop picking on him and don't

12

ever spit in his dinner again" and then he brayed seven colours of shit out of him. You should have heard the big brave bully squeal. They say revenge is a dish best served cold and he got his just deserts that day and I was left to eat my dinner in peace from then on. When I got home from school I relayed everything back to my mam and dad and they were happy that it had been sorted out.

I remember a story that my dad told me about a bully. My dad was only young at the time but there was a bloke who lived in the Burbank Street area – where Dad grew up - who thought he was hard as nails and loved it when people cowered in his presence. He was always growling and intimidating and picking on people. There was a guy who was into fitness and used to go out jogging and do a bit of boxing. Every time this bully saw the guy out jogging or exercising he would shout obscenities at him and call him names like a big girls blouse and a fairy and tell him what he would do with him, but the guy would just laugh and take no notice. One day the bully saw the guy skipping outside and thought he would teach him what being a man was all about. They drew a circle and if you stepped outside of it you lost unless you were carried out of course. It didn't take long for a crowd to gather and the bully got the whipping of his life. The guy punched his head in and the bully's inflated ego and fighting credentials were well and truly burst. Don't you just love it when bully's get a lesson like that. I wonder if it stopped him from bullying anyone else, let's hope so.

I must have been a born fighter because I was from a loving home, never beaten or abused, never deprived of anything, it was just in me. I never looked for a fight ever, it just used to come my way, follow me around, no matter how hard I tried I couldn't get away from it and by the time I was ten I'd had about 15 fights. Most of them were over after a few punches. I had a fight with a

Karate bloke's son who thought he was the business and I beat him easy. I was always a quiet lad so when people met me they didn't think I was up to much in the fighting department because I didn't boast about it like other kids did. Another fight I recall was with a lad called Bash who was your typical loud mouth, he didn't last long and I dealt with him easy. There was a bit of claret as I remember having blood on my hands and my right hand being in bad pain when I caught him on top of the head.

There was a family who lived opposite my Grandfather (Mam's dad) and the oldest brother used to hit my cousin Kevin and he'd run in crying. One day I was watching out the window and saw Kevin fighting with the younger brother and beating him, when the older brother came running out of the house and started knocking seven bells out of Kevin. The first thing that came into my head was I had to help him. I flew out and ran over and got tore straight into the older brother and gave him a good hiding. Over time I had a few fights with him and chinned him every time and it was always over Kevin fighting with his brother.

MOFFATT ROAD

My story hasn't always been about fighting. There will be lots of that later. All the stories I've mentioned so far from when I was young I was living at 4 Moffatt Road in Hartlepool. It was back in the days when your front door really was open all the time and nobody walked in and stole anything, hard to believe these days but those were the times of my childhood and you knew every family, parent, grandparent, dog, cat, uncle, auntie and friend in the neighbourhood by name. Everyone knew everybody and the community spirit was great. People were there for each other back then and if you ran out of sugar or a few tea bags all you had to do was knock on next door and they would give you them, you would do exactly the same for them when they needed anything. Imagine doing that now. People don't even know what their next door neighbours are called these days and I think that's pretty sad.

Let me share some stories of my childhood. The Weegram's lived next door for a couple of years and their son Donald was my age. We were only bairns at the time and once when his mam was having a chin wag and a cuppa at ours, they noticed that we were very quiet so went to investigate. There was Donald and I with knitting needles in our hands stripping the wallpaper off the bedroom wall! Another time we were throwing darts into the air to see how high we could throw them, a very dangerous game that could lose you an eye. Donald threw this dart and when it came down it was heading my way. I tried to get out of the way but it was like a bullet from a gun and it hit me in the back of the neck. I ran in the house in shock with a dart sticking out of my neck and got patched up by my mam. I was gutted when they moved to another part of town and had to say goodbye to my mate Donald. Another nice family moved in called Wilf and Jean Robotham with their young brood. I remember my dad and Wilf coming back from the local club where they had just won the house at the bingo and they split a wad of money which was all in one pound notes, not many people will remember the old one pound notes.

Over the road lived the Barff family and young Tommy was my age, our mam's had been friends since they were young. Tommy Snr had been in the Army and they had lived in married quarters in Germany for years so I still remember clearly the first day I clapped eyes on young Tommy. He shouted over the road to me in broken English – obviously with a bit of German slung in – that he would stab me with a knife! What a strange lad I thought but we hit it off and have been friends ever since. We even started our first day at Grange infant school together. Our mam's had took us and dropped us off and went to the local shops and we were waiting for them on the front step at home when they got back because we both done a runner. We were soon taken back to class though, much to our disapproval.

My aunt Pat was in hospital having a baby so we were looking after her other child called Gary who was still in his pram. This was the first time my mam and dad heard me swear. It was Easter and I had just brought some things in what I made at school and took them to Gary's pram to show him. His hands shot up and grabbed them out of my hands and I shouted in horror "He's got me fuckin' things". My mam laughed about that one for years.

Two doors away from me lived David Ellison and we played on the front quite a lot together. We both had small bikes what we'd fly about on. The chopper bike was the craze of the moment and everyone wanted a chopper. It was Christmas and I loved the Christmases in Moffatt Road there was just something so magical about them. I would look out the bedroom window on Christmas morning just after I'd hear Santa's bells ringing – which was my dad ringing a bell but I didn't know at the time – and look for him and expect to see him because he was just moving off the roof wasn't he? 'Can you see him' they'd say, 'No I can't see him' but I knew he hadn't forgotten me so I'd rush downstairs in my pyjamas to see what Santa had brought me. I was always buzzing with whatever I got but this year was a bit special.

'Come in the kitchen and see what you want for breakfast' but I wasn't bothered about that, 'I'll have anything' I said, 'Come in the kitchen and have a look' they insisted. I went in and was blown away by the sight that was in front of me, it was a brand new chopper bike, the one I'd dreamed about. I wanted to jump straight on it and go out for a ride but they insisted I had my breakfast first. I wolfed it down and in no time I was out on it showing it off and waiting for David to emerge so I could flash it off. When he finally came out he also had a brand new chopper bike and it was exactly the same colour as mine, you couldn't tell them apart so David's dad got some stickers made with his name on and he put them on his bike so we weren't fighting about whose was whose. I remember David going over the handle bars one day and cracking his two front teeth, blood everywhere and his teeth looked like Dracula's, he had fangs for a while until he got them sorted.

I loved football and especially liked to play in goal. Gordon Banks was in the latter stages of his England career and I idolised him. My dad would take shots at me outside on the grass and with every kick he'd say 'Save this one Banksy', 'Save that one Banksy'. I would pay football with older lads and when I moved to a new school I quickly established myself as the goalkeeper. Although I moved to a new school which was only a short bus ride away, we stayed in Moffatt Road. My first game in goal for the A team was an away game against my old school Grange and

I was the youngest player on the pitch. When we were warming up I could see people talking about me, people from my area who were older than me and didn't know me personally but knew where I lived and wondering why I was in goal for the 'other' team. It was a good game as I recall and everybody went home happy as the honours were shared in a 2-2 draw. Our team strip was light blue with a white hoop around the neck and wrist, light blue shorts and socks. It was a replica Manchester City strip and the goalkeeper's jersey was solid black. I felt so much pride whenever I pulled that jersey on.

Our arch rivals were St Teresa's, they were a great side and considered the best in the town at that time and you had to be at the top of your game to survive against them. We were away at their ground and a big expectant crowd had gathered to watch it. They were really well organised and were knocking it about lovely, making pass after pass and creating chance after chance. We were under the cosh but our defence held out, they had one cleared off the line and I pulled off a couple of good saves and we hit them on the break and scored against the run of play. Everyone was in shock as we went in at half time 1-0 up. God knows what their coach said to them at the interval but they were relentless in the second half and played us off the pitch. We defended like our lives depended on it and they were getting so frustrated because they couldn't score. Our defence were brilliant and I pulled off some one handed saves to add to their frustration. It felt like a smash and grab was on the cards but in injury time – even though there had been no injuries- they scored with the last kick of the game. It was heartbreak for us and ecstasy for them but they deserved a draw. We were consistent throughout the season – we only lost one league game - and won the league. We lost in the semi-final of the cup so just missed out on playing in the final on Hartlepool United's ground which was very disappointing for us because there were always scouts at them games looking for talent.

I was a Leeds United fan and had been since 1972 when I watched them beat Arsenal 1-0 in the FA Cup Final, the centenary final. My dad liked his football so I used to watch it all with him on the tele. Allan Clarke was my favourite Leeds player, I watched every game on 'Match of the Day' and I got the Leeds strip for my birthday with the number 8 on the back, Allan Clarke's number. Leeds United, they were something special in those days and they weren't just one of the best teams in the country, they were one of the best teams in the world.

My parents had friends at the bottom of Moffatt Road called Harry and Jean and Harry was a Sunderland fan. Every time we'd visit their house Harry would be sat in his chair and he'd grab me when I got near him, he was a rough old sod and I'm sure he used to hurt me on purpose. One of my worst days was the 1973 FA Cup Final. In the build up to the cup final Harry would torture me and wind me up constantly about how Sunderland were going to thrash Leeds and how Sunderland were a brilliant team and 'Leeds are crap' and 'Sunderland will slaughter them' and all that sort of thing I had to put up with. I couldn't wait for cup final day so I could go down their house after the final whistle and wind him up after Leeds had won. To my horror Sunderland won 1-0, it was one of the worst days of my life up to that point. Five minutes after the match finished there was a letter delivered to our house that was addressed to me and it read SUNDERLAND 1 in large letters, Leeds 0 in small letters. It was sent up by Harry who had the last laugh.

I went to see my hero's Leeds play at St James Park Newcastle United on Boxing Day in 1973 and they won with a goal by Paul

Madeley who played in defence and hardly ever scored. I read that Madeley had the ball and was taking it up the field and looking for someone to pass the ball to when he heard someone shout 'shoot'. He was a bit far out but struck the ball sweetly towards goal and it went in. Leeds won the league title that season. It was the last time they won it.

Many years later my friend Dickie was working in London with a man called Denis Wise who had a son also called Denis, who happened to be the manager of Leeds United Football Club. Old Denis arranged for us to be guests at Elland Road and what an amazing day we had. I met my old hero Allan Clarke and shook his hand. I sent a little thought up to heaven and silently said 'Did you see that Dad?', I also shook hands with other Leeds legends like Norman Hunter, Mick Jones and Paul Reaney. It was a dream day and Leeds won 2-0.

We were still living in a two bed roomed house in Moffatt Road when my dad was taken ill and had to go into hospital for some tests in which he was diagnosed with kidney failure. He then had to go for dialysis three times a week for ten hours at a time through Middlesbrough. It was hard for my parents travelling to Middlesbrough on the bus three times a week for ten hours of dialysis at a time and hardly anyone had a car in them days so a lift was out of the question. People don't realise how lucky they are these days. They trained my mam how to put my dad on the dialysis machine and they sorted a new three bed roomed house for us to move into, the back bedroom of which was made into a dialysis room for my dad to go on the kidney machine in the privacy of his own home instead of going to Middlesbrough. I was gutted to say goodbye to Moffatt Road, it was where all my memories were. All the Christmases and the excitement of waiting for Santa, slaying the dragon, chopper bike, getting drunk age five and so many more memories to mention. I loved that house but it was now time to move on. The new house was on Stockton Road right opposite a nice park called Rossmere Park.

HERO

The new house was just around the corner from my Granny Horsley's (Dad's mam) who was in her 80s by then and had seen a few changes in her time and lived through the first and second World Wars.

A couple of years earlier I used to stay at Granny's for short spells as my mam had cervical cancer and went into Newcastle General Hospital for intense radio therapy treatment and was in there for a full month. I remember going by train to visit her with my dad and mam's sister Auntie Ellen. Mam was then transferred to Hartlepool Hospital where she stayed for two more weeks and had a full Hysterectomy operation. After that she had to go for check-ups every six weeks for the first year, then every six months for two years and then once a year. Luckily the cancer never returned and Mam was given the all clear.

I was in bed one night and heard knocking at the front door; it was pretty late so I assumed it must have been urgent. I heard the man's voice and knew it was Uncle Keith, my Auntie Ellen's husband. I sneaked out of bed and listened to him talk to Mam and Dad and he was the bearer of bad news, my grandfather – Mam's dad – had just died of a heart attack. I could hear Mam crying and Dad comforting her as I crept back into bed. My Grandfather was an ex- professional boxer; he was only small and boxed as a flyweight and had 16 pro fights when he was younger. He was a chimney sweep and every time we went round he was always black with soot so my memories of him are only of him looking like he'd just brought his head out of a chimney stack which he probably had.

When I was at Granny Horsley's I made friends with Rob, Kev, Trev and Mick. Now I lived in close proximity to them we knocked about together all the time, we were football crazy and always playing footie. We played lots of other games what everyone played at the time like Kick The Tin and British Bulldogs, there wasn't just us five playing these games, lots of other kids from the area joined in, the more the merrier. These were some brilliant times that I look back upon fondly, not knowing that just around the corner my life was about to change forever.

The music from those days was great too, bands like Slade, The Sweet, Mud, Bay City Rollers, the list is endless but whenever I hear an old record it takes me back to them days, isn't it strange that music does things like that. Timeless classics when life stood still, great memories.

I used to watch Mam put Dad on the dialysis machine and sometimes she'd pamper him and put a mud pack on his face and he'd wave at me and do an Al Jolson impression. My Auntie Ellen didn't have the stomach for it as she watched Mam put Dad on the dialysis machine and as soon as she started putting these big needles into Dad's arm, she feinted and slid down the wall a naughty shade of green.

As the New Year turned into 1975 my dad was becoming ill. The kidney machine wasn't doing its work and he was losing weight. The last couple of weeks in March he started to become very ill and Mam was phoning the Hospital to keep them informed with what was happening but they were not able to admit him without a doctor's permission and Mam was calling the doctor out every other day but they wouldn't send him to Hospital. The doctor kept telling Mam to give him different drinks, some of which he wasn't allowed to have. The doctor was a useless bastard. Imagine that happening today the doctor would get done for negligence. In the end the Hospital Dad attended sent him out a card for a clinic appointment which was the only way to get him to the Hospital because the doctor wouldn't send him. When the ambulance arrived they immediately put him on oxygen, he had blacked out a few times the day before and Mam thought she had lost him, not knowing it was through lack of oxygen. As soon as they arrived at the hospital Dad was put on a trolley and wheeled in to see the doctor while Mam was told to wait in the waiting room. About ten minutes later a nurse came to see Mam with some terrible news and told her my dad had passed away. Imagine what was going through mam's mind at that moment, she will have been in shock and also very annoyed why he wasn't admitted to Hospital in the first place.

I had stayed at my Auntie Ellen's for about a week while Dad was really poorly and when she was taking me round home I was excited, I really wanted to see my dad and give him a cuddle. I loved my dad, he was my hero. I still remember Auntie Ellen say 'He's in a better place now son' but I didn't click on to what she meant, I thought by 'better place' she meant at 'home'. It was April 2nd 1975 and I went in the front room and Mam was there sat in the chair next to the fire, on her own, I looked about and said 'Where's Dad?'

Mam looked at me with a look I'd never seen before and muttered "Your dad has died son" I'll never forget those words. After a second of initial shock trying to digest what had just been said, I burst into tears and cried a river. It's hard to describe the physical pain that I felt unless you have experienced it yourself as a ten year old. The pain was unbearable. My hero was gone and life would never be the same again. The death of my father totally devastated me and I became a little introverted and went within myself for a while. I didn't want to make new friends and wanted

24

to be left alone. At that time I was just about to go into the senior school and felt like I was a loner and not a part of the crowd. I was grieving for a long time after my dad's death, these days you would probably get counselling and I think that's what I needed, to talk to a professional who knew how I was feeling and could maybe advise me, but there was nothing like that in them days so I had to deal with it myself. I just didn't feel like the same lad I used to be and became a shell of my former self. I remember one day in class one of the lads came up to me and asked if my dad had just died and I put a brave face on and said 'yes' and did my best not to cry. Then I went into senior school and stayed well away from 'who is the best fighter in first year' and kept myself to myself for a while and stayed quiet. It took about a year before I started to come out of my shell again.

I used to be scared of going into our house because I could feel this energy in there that was hard to describe to the average person who hadn't experienced it before. It was like the energy in the house was different if that makes any sense and I was sensitive to it.

I'll tell you this story and believe me this is true, I don't like talking crap and listening to people talking shit, it makes no sense to me so here goes. I was at my Uncle Jimmy's house – mam's brother - and I was asked to go round home to our house in Stockton Road and pick up a giro that was due that day for Uncle Jimmy. I wasn't bothered about doing that so I went round to 415A Stockton Road and opened the front door, sure enough there was my Uncle Jimmy's giro laid on the floor. I picked it up and put it on the electric meter next to the front door, I shut the door and went inside and would pick the giro up on the way out. Anyway on my way out, when I went to pick the giro up it wasn't there? I couldn't believe it. There was no one in the house so where had it gone? I could feel strange things were going on in the house, but for a giro to physically disappear was way beyond my imagination at the time. When I went back to my Uncle's and explained what had happened they thought I was telling them a fairy story and who can blame them. It was hard to believe wasn't it, but what else could I say, I was only telling the truth. The giro was never cashed and a couple of years later when we moved out of the house, the giro was found un-opened, under the stairs.

One night there was about eight of us in the house – Mam was at Uncle Jimmy and Auntie Pat's – and we decided to have a bit of fun with an Ouija board. The only light was coming from the coal fire and we were giving it the 'Is there anybody there' routine. I swear to god there was an almighty bang on the ceiling above our heads and everyone ran out of the house screaming in terror. I was the only one who didn't run out, I couldn't just abandon the house, I had to investigate the loud bang on the ceiling and it came from Mam and Dad's bedroom. I was absolutely terrified when I was walking up the stairs. There was nothing out of place in the bedroom but I was visibly shaken by the episode and was thinking maybe the house was haunted.

Another time I was in the house alone and went to bed and was laid there with my eyes shut when I heard footsteps coming up the stairs and the stairs were creaking with each step. I was in a living horror movie and my heart was racing. The footsteps came along the landing and stopped outside my bedroom door, I don't think I've been as frightened in all my life as I was at that moment. The first thing to come into my mind was I was going to be murdered. I froze and laid there not daring to move or make a sound but I never heard the footsteps again they mysteriously stopped. What a traumatic experience that was and I've never forgot it.

OUT THE SHELL

It had been a year since my dad passed away and I was just starting to get back to normal and come out of my shell. I ran for the school over 100 meters hurdles and made the town final. I wasn't concentrating when the gun went off and was last out of the blocks and came sixth out of eight. It didn't look like I was about to set the Athletics world alight did it. I hadn't played football for a long time either but one of the teachers asked me to play for the school team after we had a game during PE but I wasn't interested.

I got the cane for the first time after punching a lad at school. I can't remember what I hit him for but it was a cracking shot to the jaw. Then I punched a bully boy in the corridor and also punched another lad round by the lockers who had been saying stuff about me. I foolishly missed with the first shot but connected with the second and that was all it took and he folded like a ten pound note. A teacher appeared just as I had walked away but I wasn't pointed out.

The Burn Valley is a local recreational gardens that we had to walk through to get to school swimming baths and to play field sports and was frequented by many undesirables who prayed on the weak and vulnerable and many more looking to make a name for themselves by beating people up. I was walking through here when I saw two brothers staring at me so I stared back and one of them said "Who are you looking at?" so I replied "You" and one of them walked over to me menacingly but as soon as he got in striking distance I put a right hand on his chin and he hit the deck, his brother tried to surprise me but I decked him as well and put the boot into him for good measure. People soon found out I was no mug.

I had a fight with a lad a few years older than me, it was over something trivial in the street and he had a big fat bloke with him maybe that's why he was being clever because he knew he had protection. Anyway he caught me with a couple of good punches and scored first blood as my lips were bust and I could feel my eye swelling up. He had hit me with his best shots with them punches and I stayed on my feet, I had a big heart so it only made me more determined and I landed a good punch and hurt him. I knew I had him and moved in to finish it when his big fat mate grabbed me and wouldn't let me get to him. He was stood in front of me and I couldn't get past him so I was arguing with him, my blood was up and victory was only a punch or two away, then in a split second while my concentration was fixed on the fat man, the sneaky get hit me with everything he had and landed a big right hand flush on the button then ran back behind his protector. I took it no problem but I could feel my lips coming up like inner tubes. I was going mad to get at him but I couldn't get past the fat man, he was like a roundabout. I calmed down a bit and asked the lad for a fair fight but he didn't want to know and he wouldn't come out from behind Mr Roundabout. He knew he would have been smashed to bits so I reckon that was my victory.

We moved out of Stockton Road in March 1977 and went up to a caravan park in Seaton Carew where we lived for about six months and I loved it there and made a few new friends as well.

Around this time Rock n Roll had a bit of a revival with the hit TV series Happy Days and every youth club disco knocked out a few Rock n Roll records and everyone would be trying to out dance each other . All the lads used to try and act as cool as The Fonz but come on nobody was as cool as The Fonz.

My mam had being seeing a really nice bloke called Ken and he asked her to marry him, she asked me what I thought about it. Well I saw that Ken made her happy and put some stability back into her life and if she was happy then so was I, so I said "If you a want to marry him, go ahead and marry him", I did make it clear to Ken that he would be my mother's husband and not my father. Ken was happy with that. I only ever called one man my dad and I'd never do it again. No one would ever fill that man's shoes as long as I lived. Mam and Ken got married in 1977 and it was a great day, we even went up to see my old Granny Horsley who was in a nursing home then and had some pictures took with her. I had long hair and was wearing a pair of blue bell bottom trousers, a dedicated follower of fashion, I think not. It was the last time I ever saw Granny as she passed away the following year.

Ken would takes us out for day trips to seaside towns like Morecombe and Whitby and I would head for the amusements to see if there was a bar football table and if there was, I'd challenge strangers to games. I loved a game of bar football. Sometimes I'd sing Elvis songs in the back of the car while we were travelling. I loved Elvis and had a good collection of his albums. Then the news broke that Elvis had died and I was devastated, as where most of the world, the king is dead, long live the king.

One day in the caravan my mother saw a square box in my pocket that looked like a cigarette packet and said "Are those tabs in your pocket", I didn't answer her so she made me get them out and said "Right, light one up", she thought I'd just started and that it would make me sick but she realised I was a dab hand at it when I sparked it up. I started smoking her nippers out the ash tray about a year earlier, they were the non-tipped one's called Woodbines and sometimes the tobacco would hit you in the back of the throat and burn like hell and taste like shit. I managed to pack in smoking and have been a non-smoker now for twenty years and I know I will never smoke again I can't stand the smell of it now.

Talking about smells I walked in the caravan one day and this beautiful sweet aroma engulfed me, I've always had a sweet tooth and this smelt like heaven to me. My mam was making jam tarts and had just taken a pan of boiling jam off the oven and what did I do? Yes you guessed it, I stuck my finger in the boiling hot jam, what an idiot I just didn't think for one second it was going to burn the life out of my finger. I was in agony and my finger was burnt and scalded.

There was a family of sister's from Norway who lived near the caravan park, they were like tom boys and I had some good laughs with them but one day one of them was really pushing my buttons and getting on my nerves, I'd warned her constantly to stop being a nark and calling me names, well I did something I instantly regretted because I hit her. She never fell out with me over it because she knew it was her fault but I should never have hit her and I felt bad about that. They all moved back to Norway after they finished school and I never seen them but once when I was in a nightclub in the 1990s I saw her and we had a chat and she said "I've still got crooked teeth from when you hit me". I've always felt bad about that.

There was a chunky looking lad who lived on the caravan site with his mam and every time we saw each other we would just say "Alright" and that was all but we became good friends, his name was Jimmy. There was also a lad called Mick who was always begging cigarettes, or if he seen anyone smoking he would say 'save us your nipper' so we nick named him 'Nipper King'.

Nipper King had a 17 year old brother who was going in the Army called Mark who thought he was a right hard nut. Something happened with Nipper King, I think Jimmy gave him a slap, and he went to get his brother to sort him out. Jimmy and Mark fought near the club on a patch of grass that used to have swings on it and Jimmy gave him a right go and shocked Mark who thought he just had to turn up to win. No one won as they just stopped fighting but it was a good fight to watch and one of the Norwegian lasses said "you nearly had him there Jimmy", but I thought Jimmy did brilliant and he certainly impressed me with his performance. He never gave best they just stopped fighting, maybe they both knew no one would win. Another time outside the caravan club he got into an argument with a tall Welsh bird and then out of the blue, as quick as a flash 'crack', he stuck one on her chin and she went down like a baby Giraffe trying to find its legs. I was shocked but still remember it.

The day the Queen came up here for the silver jubilee celebrations I was with Jimmy at Seaton. He wound his mam up and told her that the Queen got out the car and came over to us and chatted and his mam believed him. When we moved out of the caravan down to the town centre area -Dalton Street to be exact- he used to come and visit quite regular and one time he brought my mam a paperweight from Scotland. A few years later he was on his motorbike and went through a patch of oil on the road which made his bike skid and he went straight into a lamp post. A couple of days later he died in Hospital. I have some fond memories of Jimmy. Rest in peace my friend.

The caravan park was a long way from my school, one side of the town to the other, so it was a long bus ride there and back every day. Imagine the faces of the molly coddled kids having to do that today when they are used to getting lifts and taxis.

Does anyone remember 'six of the best'? It was six lashes of the cane on your bare hands, usually three on each hand. They done away with it years ago, well they done away with a lot of things years ago and kids can't even be disciplined these days, how pathetic is that, I'm glad I grew up when it was a bit more brutal it didn't do me or my generation any harm. I got 'six of the best' for the first time when I was in second year - year 8 today – and it happened like this.

One day in Science a bunch of us where larking around with the Bunsen burners and found out that if you put the tube over the tap and turned it on, the water would fly out like a fountain. Boys will be boys. The Science teacher had a bald head with little tufts of hair at the side, I think our nick name for him was baldy basher or something like that and one of us shouted him down to the back of the class over something just to get him down there as we had a plan. As baldy basher started to walk away, one of the lads put the tube over the tap and another lad turned the tap on and as the water started squirting out everywhere I picked up the Bunsen burner and direct the flow towards the teacher and it went all over his bald head and soaked him. He turned around quickly and saw that I was the culprit and stormed down the classroom towards me while all the lads where in hysterics. He grabbed me by the collar and was screaming and shouting at me with his finger wagging in my face, I pulled his hand off my collar and pushed him away. He went to grab hold of me again and this time I pushed him away hard and told him loud and clear to 'fuck off'. When I swore at him all the class went EEEEEE in unison and my mate Terry was giggling with excitement. I stormed out of the classroom with the teacher in hot pursuit and we had a wrestling match at the top of the stairs as he was trying to drag me to the Headmaster's office, and in the heat of the wrestle I said 'fuckin' get off me' and pushed him down the stairs and done a runner. I made sure I got home at the usual time so I didn't arouse suspicion but as I got closer to home I got a few butterflies as I expected Mam saying 'what happened at school today Richard' (she always called me Richard) but nothing was said. I'm glad we didn't have a telephone in the caravan. When I eventually went back to school (I was usually playing truant) my form teacher informed me that the Headmaster, Mr Wilkinson, wanted to see me in his office. I knew what it was about but I thought maybe he wanted to see me in person and suspend or even expel me from school. He asked for my version of the Bunsen burner incident and as I was telling him my version he kept interrupting me and telling me the true version and then when he said 'you told the teacher to fuck off' I burst out laughing because I thought it sounded funny coming from him. He went ape shit with me laughing at him but after grilling me he said he was going to give me another chance. He never mentioned anything about pushing the teacher down the stairs so maybe the teacher was a little embarrassed about that bit and kept it quiet. I thought I'd got off lightly until he said he was going to cane me and I got six of the best, three on each hand. My god I was in agony and my hands were on fire, it was hard discipline but it was in place to make you behave yourself and think twice about doing it again. A few days later in Science when I saw baldy basher for the first time I was called out to the front of the class and made an example of because they (the school) didn't want anyone else doing anything similar and he gave me six of the best, three on each hand, while all the class watched and as I walked back to my chair I had a little smirk on my face, it was just a little kidology to let the class think it didn't hurt but inside I was screaming in pain because it was hurting like mad.

My mate Corbo wasn't so lucky when there was a cricket match between the teachers and the prefects. A teacher called Nuttall was batting and Corbo shouted "Nuttall go and fuck off and play with your nuts" and we were laughing hysterically. Corbo got suspended over it. If you have ever read the Skinhead books from the 1970s Corbo looked just like the lad on the front cover of Skinhead Escapes.

I was told that another lad had been saying he would take me easy so I made a mental note of it until I bumped into him, then I did one day in the Burn Valley I saw him and he had about six lads with him. I walked straight up to him and said "I heard you've been calling me names and want to fight me". I remember he was wearing a Cromby coat and Doctor Martin boots and there was snow on the ground but before he answered me I put the head on him. He slipped a little bit in the snow and was shook up so I waited until he steadied himself and hit him with a right hand which put him on his arse and volleyed him in the head and it was over in two shakes of a dog's tail. His mates were in shock and not one of them said a word to me.

I always considered myself a fighter and never ever considered myself a criminal, but I got a criminal record when I was 13 when a few of us were just having a bit of fun, and we got taken to court for wrecking farmer's haystack. You'd get a slap on the hand these days. We went potato picking to earn some money and walked for miles to get to the farmer's field but when we arrived it was deserted. Where were all the potato pickers? The only thing around was a huge haystack, which to boys of our age was like a big bouncy castle and we had fun throwing hale bales at each other. We got surrounded by the farmer and his labourer's so made a run for it and got caught and we all got locked up in the local police station. Apparently the farmer was a local magistrate and wouldn't settle out of court so we all got a criminal record because of it. Here are some edited lines of the case which appeared in the local rag at the time.

Court sequel to boys' 'horseplay' in the straw

What began as "innocent horseplay" proved to be a rather expensive past time when five youngsters came across bales of straw in a farmer's field, Hartlepool Juvenile Court heard today.

For the boys, four 13-years-olds and one aged 14 were given a 12 month conditional discharge and each ordered to pay £6 compensation when they admitted damaging the bales.

The prosecuting solicitor said his client Mr Brown, an Elwick farmer, was alerted by one of his employees on October 23.

"He drove to one of his fields where he saw this group of lads playing with his straw. They had climbed to the top and were having a great time throwing the bales to the ground and smashing them. The cost of the damage was estimated at £30," said the prosecution.

Mr White, defending three of the boys, said his clients had been out looking for work picking potatoes.

"They had no luck and were on their way home when they happened upon this haystack," he added. "As you may remember, these things hold a fascination for young lads. "They were engaged in horse play and had no intention of causing damage."

Mr Keating, for the other two defendants, said that all the boys found the straw inviting and were playing with it when caught by the farmer.

"I find the estimated cost of the straw rather puzzling, since it is usually considered worthless and burned in the field," he said.

So there you go, what a pure arsehole that farmer was getting us all a criminal record for something that was really nothing.

THROWING LEATHER

I've thrown a bit of leather in my time but the first time I remember watching a fight was with my pal Coto. It was John Conteh defending the World Light-Heavyweight title against an American Len Hutchins. Conteh won in three rounds and we were mightily impressed. I used to read the paper all the time, especially the sport in the back pages and in those days a lot of the domestic title fights were covered and I read about upcoming British title fights and the same fights would be on a programme that ran for years called Sportsnight and I'd watch them. That's how my interest in The Noble Art started. I remember watching a fighter called Dave Boy Green and I instantly liked him, he was all action and was British champ so I became a fan of Green and would read about him in the paper. He had an upcoming fight what the whole country was talking about against the former World champ John H Stracey. I read the build-up in the paper and interviews with both fighters and I recall a picture of Green in the Butcher's shop getting his steak to keep his strength up. I couldn't wait for this fight and at the allotted time I tuned the radio to the correct station and was transported to the big fight at The Royal Albert Hall. The atmosphere and anticipation, the build-up to the fight by the radio broadcast was something I'd never experienced and I had goose bumps. The fight itself was an absolute war and Green won in the tenth round and I felt like I was there. What an experience that was and I was hooked after that. I watched the recording of the fight on Sportsnight and it has stayed with me all these years and is still one of my favourite fights. I was bitten by the bug and it never left me.

I can date the move from the house in Stockton Road to the Caravan Site to March 1977, because I watched the Conteh v

Hutchins fight in Stockton Road and the Green v Stracey fight in the caravan at Seaton and both fights were in March 1977.

Boxing gyms where too far away when we lived on the caravan site but when we moved into another house I found a gym and started going. It was called the United Services Amateur Boxing Club and the head coach was a man called Duncan White. The noise and activity and smells of a boxing gym in full swing is something special, the sound of the skipping ropes twirling round at blinding speed, the punch bags swinging and being pummelled with thud after thud, the rat-a-tat of the speed ball, the grunting and groaning of other's doing floor exercises, another on the punch pads getting instructed to 'double jab, right hand and come back with a left hook', other's in the ring sparring, sweating, Vaseline smeared faces bloodied, while the coach shouts 'slip that right hand and come back with a hook to the body'. I don't know how the others felt but I loved it. There was quite a few lads in there at the time and always somebody in the ring sparring and you found out that boxing was an art, you didn't just go in there and throw leather and hope for the best because if you did you would soon find yourself on the floor in pain. I asked a few of the lads I knocked about with if they fancied coming to the gym, some of them where tough lads on the streets but I wanted to see how tough they were in the squared circle. We wouldn't hold back and would hit each other with our best shots, it was then that the older lads who I hung around with realised how tough I was, I could take it as well as give it. There were many times I saw lads who had a reputation on the streets come into the boxing gym and think they were going to be the bees knees, they'd get put in the ring with someone who knew the basics and they'd take a pasting and you'd never see them again. You see our coach Duncan didn't want to waste his time with someone who didn't want to know, that's why you sparred pretty quickly and took your lumps and bumps and if you come back and wanted more, then you were worth spending time on. He'd take the gloves off you after sparring and you'd be banged up or bloodied and he'd say "That's what it's all about" with a hint of a smirk on his face. An older lad called Tommy used to take all the new recruits like myself and put us through training drills, my god I didn't know how hard you had to train, they were Hellish sessions and those sessions alone would stop people coming never mind the pastings in the ring. Things like this sorted the men out from the boys. I had been going for few months and would soon be getting my medical to allow me to box but something was about to derail my boxing baptism.

I was suffering quite badly with pains in my legs so Mam made an appointment for me to see the doctor and I was diagnosed with Osgood-Schlatters disease. Basically I was growing too fast and it usually strikes during puberty and is more common in boys. It is inflammation of the bone where the thigh muscles attach to the lower leg, the symptoms are pain, tenderness and swelling below the knee. I had to wear bandages on my knees for six months and have my boot heel built up by quarter of an inch. I wasn't allowed to do any physical activity for 12 months and the doctor sent a letter to my school to excuse me from PE for a full year. I couldn't believe it, just when I was going to have my first boxing fight I was hit with this. I remember thinking 'why me'. I went to the boxing gym and told Duncan the bad news and he was as gutted as I was but I said 'mark my words I'll be back'.

I spent a lot of time at the youth cub with my friends and Thursday night was always disco night. Saturday Night Fever and Grease where the big thing at the time and I'll admit I went to see Grease at the pictures but so did everyone else because there were long queues every night, and you'd be surprised at how many so called 'hard' lads were stood in the queue waiting to see Grease. On disco nights people would wear black leather jackets and act cool and try to pull the birds, other people thought they were The Fonz, funny now looking back. There was a couple of brothers who went to dancing classes and the DJ would clear the floor for one record, while they and two girls would dance to the song Greased Lightning, the two brothers thought they were Danny Zuko and the two females were dolled up like Olivia Newton John. Sometimes there would be fighting but mostly it was trouble free. Flared trousers, short and long leather coats, denim jackets, doctor martins and Dublin boots were the fashion of the time. I would earn a few extra quid at school letting a class mate punch me in the jaw for ten pence a punch and he absolutely loved it. I can still see the smile on his face when a punch made a loud noise which sometimes had us both laughing, him more than me.

The music scene was changing with bands like The Sex Pistols and The Clash and Punk Rock exploded into our ears and our lives. My pal bought the album Never Mind The Bollocks and I used to go round and listen to it and we'd laugh at some of the swear words and then he dyed his hair and everyone laughed at him and then other people started dying their hair and before long everyone was at it. One night at the disco the DJ put a punk rock song on and my pal was on the dance floor doing the pogo on his own, people laughed at first, I don't think they knew what else to do as he was the first person they'd seen do it but before long the dance floor was full of punk rockers doing the pogo and the punk explosion swept through our town. I started knocking about with a different crowd, the punk crowd. I used to wear a padlock and chain around my neck like Sid Vicious and so did my mate Measor who also got a Sid Vicious tattoo on his arm. One night outside the youth club Measor had a one-on-one fight and almost got choked with his padlock and chain, I didn't want that happening to me so I took mine off and never wore it again. I remember sat in the front room at home and the ten o'clock news came on and the first story was that The Sex Pistols bass player Sid Vicious had killed himself and my mam's husband Ken said 'The bloody idiot'.

I went to the hairdressers and got a suede-head cut, which was then dyed blond and had question marks dyed into it. I was over the moon with it and it was totally different to what everyone else had and I didn't half get some funny looks from people. When it grew out I didn't get it done again but I wish I had my photo took then so I could look back at it and have a laugh.

We started going to a youth club which was full of bikers and there was always fighting, we introduced punk rock up there and they hated us for it. When the DJ would put a couple of punk records on for us we'd get drinks threw on us as we were doing the pogo and it would kick off and usually once a fight started everyone would get involved because it would be punks versus bikers. I did the unthinkable and started knocking off one of the biker's girlfriends and a few weeks later he found out about it and came looking for me with a couple of Gorillas. I was coming out of the town one Saturday afternoon when they spotted me and I thought 'this is it' and instead of running away, I started walking towards them. I think he was a bit shocked when he saw I wasn't frightened. He offered me out and I said yes. I was with my mate Measor and as we looked about for a place to fight, I looked at one of his mates who I knew was a handy lad, looked down at his Dublin boots and cheekily said, "I suppose I'll be getting a taste of them will I" and he nearly set about me in the street but there were too many people about. We went to some wasteland which ironically is now a doctor's health centre, and I calmly took off my denim jacket, slowly unbuttoning each button, nice and calm and looking at him letting him know he was making a mistake. The wasteland ran along a busy street and there were people all over but we were getting it on regardless so I handed Measor my coat and we squared up. He came at me and I snapped his head back with a jab. I was moving around him, side-stepping and giving him angles and hitting him with jabs and he couldn't land a punch on me. As soon as they saw me move, one of his mates said in a surprised voice, 'A boxer'. It was like taking candy from a baby. His eyes were watering off my jabs and when he tried to take me to the floor I side-stepped out the way. I was softening him up with the jab before I unleashed the right hand but before that happened a Policeman arrived on the scene, alerted by frightened old women walking past, the other lads bolted but he was only interested in the fighters. He threatened to lock us up and gave us both a talking to for a while and got the full story from us both why we were fighting in the first place. Then he asked for our names and addresses, the biker said he was 19 and when he asked my age and I said I was 14 the biker got a shock and said if he knew I was only 14 he wouldn't have fought me. The copper cautioned us both and sent us on our way.

About eight of us punk rockers jumped into a transit van and headed to a disco out of town. We were expecting to make friends but were met with hostility and they started barging into us on the dance floor and knocking us flying and there was a lot of tension in the air. There must have been ten times more of them than us and we were completely outnumbered but we'd had enough of the dance floor antics and it all kicked off and spilled outside. We were outnumbered like Davey Crocket at The Alamo. One of our boys ran to the van and got a length of thick chain and started wrapping it round their heads. The Police arrived and stopped the fighting but our van had been damaged and one of the tyres slashed. After the cops got the story and realised we were the innocent party they said if we changed the tyre and left straight away we wouldn't get locked up and there would be no charges, we didn't have to be told twice and once the tyre was changed we were out of there like a bat out of hell. The song 'Babylon's Burning' by The Ruts reminds me of that night, what an adrenaline buzz that was. I still had plenty of fights at the biker youth club and once one lad started fighting it always turned into a mass brawl like in the old cowboy films. Punk Rock didn't last too long but it was great while it did and those were good days.

ROCKY'S DEBUT

In my final year at school I hardly ever went and couldn't wait to leave and one time in the classroom I said to the lads "I'm sick of this I think I'll go" and the lads dared me, so I pushed the table away and walked out during a lesson. The teacher shouted "Horsley where do you think you're going", "Horsley get back here", I just ignored him and kept walking and he never came after me. Another time I arrived home and Mam said "How was school today" I replied "Ok" and she said "Why was the school board man here today asking why you hadn't been for the past two months" I just started laughing, I was in my last year so it made no difference to me anyway. I wasn't suddenly going to get hit with a thirst for knowledge and want to get my grades for University. My University was the school of life what you couldn't learn in books. I was never really a school person, they say they're the best days of your life, I wouldn't say they were mine.

I left school age15 and my first job was with a local builder who renovated houses. The hours were long and if truth be told all he wanted was a young dogsbody he didn't have to pay much. I worked for him for a week and he said I wasn't what he was looking for. I thought he was an arrogant wanker and if I was a bit older I would have chinned him for sure.

I went back to the boxing gym and Duncan was happy to see me, I made good on my promise that I would be back. There was a very good boxer in the ring shadow boxing, he'd been an amateur for years and within 12 months he'd be a professional. I had sparred with him before but was always on the receiving end. I wanted to find out if I could hold my own and asked him to spar and he said "sure". When the bell rang I went straight at him and let go with a ferocious intent which I think surprised him, but he came back at me just as hard, neither of us would give an inch and we traded full blooded shots, toe-to-toe, and could have fought in a telephone booth. After two rounds, Duncan stopped the sparring before we "kill each other". I left that session satisfied that I could hold my own with a very good experienced boxer and I hadn't even had an amateur fight yet.

I started work on a Government scheme doing Sea Defence down at Middleton beach. It was hard laborious graft but it built my strength up for boxing. It involved filling up wire cages called Gabions with bricks and rocks and stacking them along the beach, building a sea wall. Once one level was completed then another was added, and another, and another, I think there was about eight levels altogether. It was hard carrying the rocks and bricks up the beach but you got used to it. The gaffer used to call me Rocky and would say "This will build your strength up for fighting, Rocky".

After eight hours of that everyone would go home and relax but I would go to the boxing gym and train. I walked to work every morning and would walk past the famous old ship The Warrior that was being restored at the docks. One day I was on the back of a workmate's bike and my foot got stuck in the spokes and we both went over the handle bars and I got a fat lip. I had my first fight a few days later and thought it might be called off but Duncan had a word with the doctor and when I was getting a medical, the doctor looked at my fat lip and said "what's that a cold sore" with a smirk on his face. I fought well and won on points, although I was a little tired in the last round and took a few shots from my more experienced opponent I still got my hand raised in victory and what a good feeling it was.

There was an Army bloke who came to the gym for a couple of weeks and he wanted to spar with everybody, "I box for the Army" blah, blah, blah. Every time he got in the ring he would go at it hard and not pull his punches, this guy was out to hurt people, trying to prove a point or something. I knew I would be in with him soon and I wanted to get in and test myself with him. I knew what to expect when the time came to spar, and from the bell he didn't hold back and let the punches fly. I was boxing him and using my brain and noticed if I jabbed him to the body he dropped his left hand a little. I kidded him with a pretend jab to the body and his hand came down to parry it, but while his jaw was exposed I exploded a right hand off it and his eyes rolled and he went down in the corner of the ring. He took a bit to revive and the coach had a worried look on his face. I got a bit of a ticking off in private by the trainer who said he could see what was going to happen before it did. There were some good boxers in our gym and I took my fair share of punishment but it's all a part of the learning process. I'd watch guys like Ken Foreman who had silky smooth skills and the best jab I'd ever seen, he was a southpaw as well and when I sparred with him I knew I was in with a quality lad. Another was Big Ronnie and I'd be banged up with a black eye or bust nose after a session with him but I loved it. Another lad was Micky who had over 100 fights and was a cracking fighter. I remember he hit me with a left hook on the jaw just as the bell sounded and I felt everything drain from my legs. I had to go another couple of rounds but that's how you learn to suck it up and fight through it and get experience.

I was entered in the boxing championships and in the first regional round at Sunderland I won my fight which progressed me to the next round at Darlington and I won again and with it I became North East champion at 75kg in the 16 year old class which was known as Class B. I was now through to the National quarter-finals were I fought a lad from Manchester who was in the final the previous year. Well the night before the big fight a workmate who I'd known years, was getting engaged and having a party at a club called The Wagga which has long since been demolished. I went to the party with the intentions of going home early but I ended up having a good drink and had a bit of a hangover when I woke up. Anyway in the fight, I was doing well and thought I won the first round with cleaner punches and doing more of the work. The other lad was a counter-punching southpaw who had that kind of style to make anybody look bad. I recall at the end of the first round Duncan saying "He's scared of you" and so I continued where I left off in the second round, but with the awkwardness of his style, we came together and clashed heads and I thought I heard someone throw water in the ring but then the ref shouted 'stop boxing' and sent my opponent to a neutral corner and I realised it wasn't water but my blood and I was unfortunate to get a split eyebrow caused by the head clash. The ref took one look and stopped it and I got six stitches put in it by the doctor, while the other lad went on to win the title.

After the Christmas break I returned in late January with a points win over a lad from Aycliffe called Harty. I took a few hard shots on my eyebrow but it held firm, mind you I had a peach of a shiner the next day. I recall walking down York Road and bumping into our Kevin and a couple of his pals and he said "What happened to you", I told him I'd fought the night before and won and he said "You hard bastard". I fought Harty again and he hit me with a right hand and I almost went over but I grabbed him round the waist and held him until my head cleared. I dropped him in the first with a combination against the ropes and stopped him in the second round. I also fought a big lad about 6ft 5in which was really tall for a Light-Heavyweight, he was talking in the dressing room about how good he was and my club mate

47

said "Have you heard him bulling himself up". He had a very long reach and after two rounds Duncan said to me "you are going to have to knock him out this round to win" so from the bell I pushed him back and got him on the ropes and hit him with body shots, then I caught him with a beautiful right uppercut which almost lifted him out his boots and the fight was stopped.

I fought the best Light-Heavyweight in the country and four times National champion Gary Crawford, it was in the championships and the winner went on to the finals. He was by far the best I'd ever fought and was a class act. His jab was like getting hit with a right hand, so accurate with so much power behind it. I tried to match him with the jab but I wasn't as successful. He had been boxing since he was seven. I got caught on the ropes and he hit me with some lovely shots flush on the chin, I hadn't been hit as hard as that before but my legs held out and I was still on my feet. He looked at me with the strangest look I'd seen in a ring, the look said 'why haven't you gone down'. He did catch up with me with a big right hand that landed on my throat and the ref gave me a count. As he was counting I said to him "He hit me in the throat" and it felt like my Adams apple was broke and I was gesturing to my throat when he waved it off and stopped it. Crawford went on to win the title. I followed his pro-career – he fought under the name Crawford Ashley - and was over the moon he became a triple champion, European, British and Commonwealth and he won a Lonsdale belt outright, and also had three World title fights. He was a class act.

I'd been out of the gym for a few months and when I went back in Duncan said to me "I was going to come to your house and see you after the gym I'm glad you are here. Will you fight Glenn McCrory on Thursday in Consett", I had been nowhere near a gym in months and he was asking me to fight McCrory on his own club show. If I had been in shape I would have said yes straight away. If any matchmakers had any last minute problems they would phone Duncan and he would usually pull them out the shit. I said "Did they offer any money" and he said no. I said I'd fight him if they offer me some money but that was the last I heard of it.

I went up to the Newcastle area somewhere and fought a tough Geordie called Ronnie Nesbitt, I was 17 and he was 30. Some people were videoing the show but I've never seen a copy of the fight. He was a strong man and hard as nails, I boxed most of the fight on the back foot and was hitting him as he came in. He would just plough forward all the time and never took a step back. I hit him with lots of jabs and sometimes I'd stand and trade with him but that was his game and I didn't want to fight his fight, so I moved around and made him eat my jab. I was tired in the last round and he came on strong, throwing everything at me but I was never troubled. It was a good fight and the crowd loved it. Duncan couldn't make that fight but another coach called Ernie was in my corner. A few days later in the gym I heard him telling someone about it and he was saying "what a fight". It made me feel good hearing that.

In the championships I got to the final at Light-Heavyweight and fought a very good lad called Eddy Ellwood. I watched him warming up shadow boxing and he looked very fast, he'd been around a while and had fought abroad. We were trading punches and he caught me with a few head shots and the ref gave me a standing count and while he was doing this I protested "why am I getting a count I'm not even hurt" but he took no notice. We went straight at it again trading shots, I missed with a hook that would have took his head off if it found the target, we clinched and he was breathing heavily, I knew he was gambling on an early finish and if I weathered the storm he'd blow himself out and I'd stop him. He rallied off another combination of punches while I was backed against the ropes, some of which hit my arms, and the ref shouted 'stop boxing' and stopped the fight. I asked the ref why he stopped it because I wasn't in any danger and had never been hurt but he just waved me away. I was gutted and felt dejected. I told Duncan I was packing it in and he said 'don't worry I'll get you a return fight' so I held him to his word and sure enough he got me a return fight. The day of the fight I had butterflies thinking about what lay ahead. I knew what to expect this time, he was a good boxer and very fast for a big man, he was sharp with his combinations but I felt I could soak them up, make him miss as much as I could and hopefully he would gas. That was my plan anyway and I got weighed in and waited for Eddy to arrive. I saw him come in and he came straight over to me and said he was feeling unwell so the fight was off. It was an anti-climax but there's no use crying over spilt milk. I became friends with Eddy, what a nice bloke he was. He went into body building and was very successful at it winning lots of titles, including the Professional Mr Universe five times in a row. He is the owner and manager of a great gym called Xtreme Fitness.

I fell out of love with boxing for a while and spent a lot of time drinking down the town with my mates getting hammered. I would bump into the boxing lads who would ask me to go back to the gym but I was happy doing what I was doing for the moment and wasn't ready to go back to the gym, I would know myself when I was ready. At the time a lot of people were tooled up with homemade truncheons so not to be outdone I stuck one in my waistband, it was one end of a pair of Nunchakus. It was more of a novelty thing than anything else as my fists where my weapons and always have been and I have never used a weapon in a fight, ever. I was out on the lash one night and had my home made truncheon in my waistband and someone must have clocked it and maybe thought it was a gun or something else sinister and the next thing I know I was getting arrested for possession of an offensive weapon. I was taken to court and received a £50 fine.

I went to Bradford to watch Hartlepool play and some of the lads had home-made coshes. When we got in the ground they mistakenly put us in with the Bradford supporters and a massive fight broke out, there was that many people fighting it was hard to tell who was who and it took an army of cops to bring it under control, there was lots of arrests but I wasn't arrested, although I did put a few on their arse.

Then one night I was walking to the youth club and a couple of lads were walking past and one of them motioned to me to 'come on' meaning he wanted to fight so I punched him and he ran off with his mate, they ran straight to the Police station and reported me for assault. I got locked up and charged and had to go to court where I was remanded for seven days to Low Newton. The following is edited highlights from the local paper,

Exchange of words led to assault by youth

An exchange of words quickly led to a case of assault. Horsley was walking along Grange Road and two youths passed walking in the opposite direction, words were exchanged which quickly led to a case of assault. Horsley thought the youth he assaulted wanted to fight him. "The words 'come on' were spoken by the unfortunate victim and I do not know whether he wanted a fight, but it was taken that way. This wasn't a mugging or unprovoked attack it was something that came out of words exchanged" said the defending solicitor Mr Gray. The Magistrates remanded Horsley to Low Newton while social enquiry reports were drawn up.

After a week in that shit hole I was glad to see my mam in the court room. The jury went out to consider their verdict, I had a brilliant social enquiry report which swayed it for me, the judge said before he read that report I was getting six months, but because I had such a good report I deserved another chance. I was relieved to hear those words and received 180 hours of community service.

Mam's husband Ken was brought up the old fashioned way and couldn't understand the way I went on. One night when my mate Coto stayed over we left the lights on all night and it was the straw that broke the camel's back. Ken went mad with me and we had a big argument in the kitchen and I ripped my shirt off and offered him outside. Mam came in and broke it up before I dropped him and he told me to 'get out of his house' which I duly did after some choice words. I got my gear together and went to live with my girlfriend's parents, there were already six of them under the same roof and now there were seven.

I did my community service which seemed to take forever but eventually I done the full 180 hours. That is four and a half weeks of unpaid work at 40 hours per week but at least I wasn't behind bars. I had been waiting for ages for the Larry Holmes v Gerry Cooney fight so I got up at the allotted time during the night and tuned the radio in and off I was, ringside in the heat of Las Vegas. Reminded me of the days when I listened to Dave Boy Green and others. I was a Larry Holmes fan and thought he was so underrated by the boxing experts. He is certainly in the top ten Heavyweights of all time and had the best jab. I started training at the professional gym and would spar with a good pro called Phil Gibson who was straight out of the Jake LaMotta mould. I also went to see Duncan White and told him I wanted a fight and would he get me fixed up. I didn't have to wait too long before I was matched with a bloke in his early 30s and we fought at Peterlee Leisure Centre, my mate Eddy Ellwood was also on the bill. Anyway I wasn't boxing that well and Duncan was giving me a right old tongue lashing between rounds. In the third round I got a salty taste of snot in my mouth and looked at his nose and I could see it had snot on it, I had his snot in my mouth and I almost spewed up. It spurred me into action and I hit him with a hard furious combination and he went down and took a count and got up. The ref waved it to continue and I hit him again and his legs went to jelly and the bell rang. I won a unanimous decision and a few weeks later I fought a hard nut from Aycliffe called Wilkinson, he had beat some good lads on the circuit. We had a stare down back stage and he looked up for it, he was mid 20s with shoulders like a barn door so I knew he carried power. He caught me with some big shots in the first round and my face felt like I'd had a stroke. I knew I'd lost the first but was determined to win the second, it was hard going and the punches were hurtful but I took them and traded with him and went forward and put him on the back foot. It was all riding on the last round and both of us gave it everything we had and it was anyone's fight until I caught him flush on the chin with a lead right hand and he hit the deck with a thud to loud cheers from the fans. This lad had balls and he got up and took the count and the ref waved it back on. He back peddled and I went after him and the bell rang. What a hard fight, tough and brutal but I won a split decision and my eye was closed shut the next morning. That fight was videoed but I've never seen it.

I was also the proud father of a baby girl called Jill Louise and I'll never forget the feeling of being a father it was better than winning the lottery. I was now living over the road from my friend, the British lightweight champion George Feeney and I'd go out running most mornings with him. He would do eight miles and I would do four. I ran and trained with him for his fights with World champion Ray 'Boom Boom' Mancini and Olympic champion Howard Davis. Sometimes we'd chat while running and tell stories and I remember one was about the great Rocky Marciano who had Italian parents. Well George's manager was a fantastic bloke and character called Dennie Mancini (I remember answering the phone once in the gym and it was Dennie pretending to be Ray Clark from the British Boxing Board of Control and he need to speak urgently with George Bowes?). Denny's family was Italian and they had pubs in London and in one of the pubs Denny announced that the great Rocky Marciano would be paying a visit tomorrow night. No one believed him. Rocky was in London at a function of some sort and called at Dennie's pub and they reckon people's jaws dropped in disbelief when he walked in and I can just imagine the look on people's faces. That was one of the stories on our morning runs I thought I'd share with you.

My pal George won a Lonsdale belt outright but in his last fight in Germany for the European title he got robbed of the win even though he decked the champion twice. He developed a detached retina which resulted from that fight and even if he had won, it would have been his last fight anyway as the doctor advised him to retire and that's what he did. I went to visit him at the Sunderland eye infirmary after his operation and took him a couple of boxing books. George was great fighter who was unlucky not to be European champion.

Duncan had entered me in the ABA championships but wanted me to go in at Middleweight because he thought I'd have a better chance. I was a teenage Light-Heavyweight and growing all the time so why would I want to lose a stone in weight, it didn't make sense, it would bloody kill me but I said I would try. I was training hard and was sharp in sparring and felt fit but I was struggling to get the weight off and I wasn't going to weaken myself in the process. On the morning of the ABAs I was still five pounds over and I thought 'that's it I'm not doing it' so I didn't go. If I had gone in at my normal weight it would have been no problem and I would have fought Glenn McCrory in the regional rounds. I don't know if anything went on behind the scenes so I went in at a different weight to McCrory or that Duncan thought McCrory would beat me so wanted me to switch weight classes to avoid him, I'll never know but I ended up not throwing a punch in the ABAs and took time out from the ring because I needed a break from it.

GIVEN AWAY

Life was changing all the time and I was living at my Auntie Ellen's and sharing a bedroom with my cousin's Kevin and Kenny, when one day Auntie Ellen was looking through some old photographs and pointed to one and said to me "That's your sister there", I knew I had two sister's but had never seen a picture of any of them and now here I was looking at one of them. I couldn't stop thinking about it over the next week or so, 'what do they look like now', 'do they know they have a brother', 'would they like to meet me' and things like that where going through my head. My mam got in touch with their mother Violet - my birth mother – and told her that I wanted to meet my sister's so she arranged it and I went and met them both. It was a surreal feeling meeting my flesh and blood for the first time, I didn't know how they would react so I didn't say too much as I didn't know what to say. Both had partners and children of their own so I didn't want them to feel like I was interfering so I didn't go and see them as much as I'd liked.

I went to our Jackie's this particular day and she was going to visit her mother Violet - my birth mother – and asked if I would go with her so I said yes. I had never seen Violet before and not even saw a picture of her so I hadn't a clue what she looked like. I asked Jackie to phone her mother to let her know I'd be coming along but she said no, she wanted to surprise her. Anyway we arrived and went in the front room and Jackie had this grin on her face because she knew what was coming. I watched Violet say to Jackie under her breath 'who's that', meaning who was I. Jackie said out loud "That's our Richard" and when it dawned on her she let out a yelp and ran into the kitchen. Jackie was smiling her head off. Violet composed herself and came back in the room and said "Jaqueline you should have phoned and I would have made myself look decent". We had a cuppa and a bit of a chin wag and left.

My mam Brenda had known Violet since they worked together at Cameron's Brewery in the bottling department around 1958. One day my mam was walking down the street and she bumped into Violet, they hadn't seen each other for years. Violet was pushing a pram with two little girls in it and they had a chat. Violet asked Mam if she had any children but Mam said no, she did have a child a few years previous but the infant had died at six months old and she couldn't have any more children, Mam was still grief stricken over her baby. Violet said "I'm pregnant again but I don't want it. You can have this if you want it" and Mam said "If you are serious Violet yes I do want it I would love to have it", and that is how I came to be 'adopted' but I wasn't officially adopted, I was given away. When Violet was due out of hospital six days after giving birth to me, my mam and dad where there to pick me up and on the way home in a taxi they dropped Violet off. It was the best thing that could have happened to me and I had a good upbringing so Violet did the right thing for me.

My dad's sister Ruby was psychic and she made a prophecy one day when she was visiting them. She knew they had lost a baby and couldn't have any more children but she said "I'm going to tell you both something and you might think I'm crazy, but I can see a pram outside your front door. Mark my words a baby is coming from somewhere for you two". A couple of years later my mam bumped into Violet and the rest is history.

My two sisters Debbie and Jackie didn't have a loving childhood and were often smacked. Their mam and dad drank most nights at home and were constantly fighting and shouting at each other at the top of their voices. Violet would get her hair done on Friday's and by Saturday morning it had been rove out. She wasn't so innocent she was a promiscuous woman and I think Violet done Jack's head in and that's what turned him to drink. One day Jack got home at lunch time to find a letter waiting for him off Violet, it said she had left him and she went off to live with another man, a bus driver, whom she married. When he got home from work that evening he told the girls that their mother had left and wasn't coming back. Imagine that, it's hard to get your head around. The girls will have felt abandoned off their mother but at least they still had their dad. In later life Jackie said to Debbie "Richard was the lucky one getting adopted".

We found out that there wasn't just the three of us as we had thought and that Violet had given birth to a baby boy in 1959 and had him adopted. I searched for years without success to find my brother. I even went on the TV programme Surprise Surprise back in the 1980s and went on a part of the show called Searchline, making an appeal to find my brother, all to no avail. I was sick of getting asked by people 'Did you find your brother' only having to say 'No' to them.

I found out he was called John and was born on 8th August but that was the only information I had for all them years, every time I searched I hit a brick wall. A lot of the time it was just so frustrating. One day my mam had a letter through the door and when I went to see her she said "Have you been threatening the woman at the Durham Diocese", I said 'no what are you talking about' and she showed me the letter. I must have sounded threatening because I was so frustrated at the lack of information because they have a privacy policy they are not allowed to breach. I actually got a copy of his birth certificate in 2012 and it felt like I was getting somewhere and it proved to me that he was real and I did have a brother.

A year later 2013 I got in touch with After Adoption and was assigned a case worker. I gave them all the information I had and left it with them. We exchanged e-mails and phone calls but they are not allowed to divulge any information and I got a phone call to say they found a man that matched all the information I had given them. They had wrote to him and told him the story and that his brother was looking for him and would like to meet him etc. I was buzzing. I had to wait a few weeks and there was still no news, maybe he didn't want to know or maybe he was having a long think about it and wasn't ready yet or needed more time. My mind was boggling with it all. My wife Wendy went through it all with me and was as excited as I was, she was hoping for a happy ending. He was on the electoral role at that house until 2006 and he hadn't moved anywhere else and nobody else was down as living at the property. When there was no reply they wrote to him again and said the same things in this letter. They told me they couldn't write again because it would be seen as harassment so were hoping he might reply to this. As the weeks went by there was still no reply and I was thinking he didn't want to know or he would have been in touch by now. If he didn't want to know I would rather he said and then I'd know to forget it and say at least I tried. The waiting was doing my head in and as the weeks came and went there was still no reply. I messaged my old mate Eddy Ellwood and asked him if he knew a man who fitted the description because he was from the collieries and so was my brother, but Eddy didn't know him but what he did say was "Why don't you put an appeal on Facebook you never know who might see it" and that's what I did. It wasn't on very long and my old pal Vulture phoned me and said "Why don't you get in touch with Fraser, he does stuff like that for a living. He will find your brother". I hadn't seen Fraser for years and didn't know he was into that kind of thing. I spoke with Fraser on the phone and gave him the little details I had and he said he'll be in touch. Less than an hour later he phoned me and said "Out of all the people in the country, only one matched your information and he lives in Easington Colliery. I'm going up there now to knock on his door". My god I couldn't believe how fast he found him and all the years of frustration would soon be over one way or another. Fraser knocked on his door but there was no answer. He didn't want to leave with no information so he knocked at next door. The neighbour said that John had died in 2006 after falling down the stairs drunk and smashing his head at the bottom causing a severe Haemorrhage to the brain. He had laid there for a couple of days before a neighbour noticed he hadn't been taking the dog for a walk so they phoned the cops. When The Police went in the house they found John at the bottom of the stairs dead and the dog by his side, what a tragic end. When Fraser phoned me and said "It's not good news I'm afraid" I thought he was going to say he had spoken to him and he wasn't interested in meeting but when he told me what happened I felt like I'd just been hit with a hammer. Then I started to grieve for John even though I'd never met him, it was the closing of the story that had been playing an on off role in my life since 1984 and it was finally at the journey's end. Wendy and I done some investigating and found out that John had a girlfriend but they were split up at the time of his death and she hadn't seen him for a couple of weeks prior. We got her phone number and spoke to her a few times and got lots of information from her about him. He knew he was adopted but he didn't know he had a brother and two sisters. His ex-girlfriend said John would definitely have met me and he would have been thrilled to bits to know he had a brother. She also said he was a Leeds United fan and would go on the train to their club shop and buy Leeds T-shirts and other merchandise. I obtained the only known photograph of him and he was wearing a Leeds United T-shirt. It was an amazing feeling to see picture and see what he looked like and I got a copy of it. The things we missed out on talking about but not every story has a happy ending. At least I could finally put it to bed now.

MEDOMSLEY

I had moved out of our Ellen's and had a flat near the town and was drinking and partying with the lads most of the time and basically just enjoying myself. One night I was on my way home the worse for wear and tripped and fell into a shop window and it smashed everywhere. I managed to get up and stagger along the street before the police picked me up, took me to the station and charged me with criminal damage. When I was at court over it I was ordered to pay something stupid, I can't recall how much exactly, I know the window wasn't worth that much. I didn't pay a penny of it and ended up back in court over it and told the judge I had no intention of paying a penny and he gave me 90 days inside. I went to Low Newton for the first week and while I was there I saw my mate Cliffy who was doing six months and we'd chat about the good nights we had on the town. I would see him going to work in the gardens on a morning and I'd shout a few things at him from my cell and he'd laugh his head off. Later that year he would be dead after a fight outside a nightclub.

I was sent to Medomsley Detention Centre to do the rest of my sentence. Detention Centre's were vile horrible places on the lines of an Army boot camp and all Detention Centre's were eventually closed down because they were too brutal. It was physical and mental torture all the way and everything had to be done at a hundred miles an hour. Most people would pick prison over these places and the idea was on the lines of a short sharp shock. Sometimes it worked and sometimes it didn't. To be employed there you had to be pure evil or you weren't cut out for the job. The worst screw in the place was the gym orderly called Onslo who was a right sadistic bastard and I had a run in with him on my first day. As soon as you arrived he would in-still fear into you and he was marching the new lads to his office, me being one of them, and he pushed me hard in the back and screamed "Get a move on" but I didn't move any faster because that would mean I was dancing to his tune and I wasn't going to do that, so he went berserk. He grabbed me and slammed me against the wall to knock the wind out of me, then he smashed my head off the concrete wall a couple of times and then the punches started raining down on me. I was cool as a cucumber and I just rolled with his punches and they had no effect on me at all. One of the screws who was there watching it all was called Bulldog and his face was a picture when he saw the way I handled the situation and I think it unnerved him a bit where I was concerned. Onslo was screaming at me and I was just nice and calm saying yes sir, no sir. The new lads who watched it were in total shock but for the lads who saw it from their windows it was an everyday occurrence to them. I didn't know it but I had already made my mark when he and the others saw he couldn't hurt or frighten me.

At six o'clock every morning the screws would shout 'Fall In' and you had to be out of your bed and down the stairs to the end of the corridor to be counted and you had to be there ASAP or you would face the consequences. Sometimes people would be so tired they couldn't get out of bed and the screws would drag them out and kick them all over while screaming and shouting at them. Everyone had to be clean shaven every morning and you only had a couple of minutes to do it. One morning another evil screw called German was handing the razors out and I'd just put the foam on my face and he shouted 'Razors in NOW' so I just wiped the foam off my face and gave him it back. I got away with it while other people wouldn't have.

I had only been in a couple of days when I had a run in with the 'Daddy', who was the hardest lad in the place. Everyone knew a confrontation was on the cards and all the Hartlepool lads were buzzing they had someone to look after them. It was hard to have a proper fight in there because you were watched 24-7 there wasn't any time you weren't being looked over by an evil screw, apart from when you were asleep but you were too tired then. I had been in a works party in the gardens and we were all going to wash the mud and crap off our wellies but there was a long queue and the 'Daddy' was stood washing his wellies with the hosepipe while everyone watched him and he seemed to be taking his time, was he taking the piss. I walked to the front of the queue and snatched the hosepipe out his hand and grabbed him by the scruff of the neck and threw him up against the wall and told him I was going to rip his fuckin' head off. The screws were on us in a flash and broke it up. I had made my move and everyone was talking about it and he said he wanted to fight me but it was all talk, I was the new 'Daddy'.

Out of the blue the next day I was given a cushty job in the stores with the radio blaring out every day. There was a long list to get a job in the stores and I had jumped the queue. No more getting covered in shit in the gardens for me.

During lunch they shouted out your name if you had any mail and you would go and get it one at a time when called. This day the big ugly screw known as Bulldog was doing the mail and shouted my name and my mam had sent a Boxing News in for me and Bulldog let it be known that you are not allowed anything through the post but he'd allow me to have this one but no more so I had to stop getting them sent in. Did I stop? No I didn't and Bulldog kept giving me them with a scowl on his face. The first few days I was in we were lined up in a corridor and I could hear a growl from the lad behind me. I turned round and he was massive but I said 'Who the fuck are you growling at I'll rip your head off next time I hear that do you understand' you should have seen the shocked look on his face when he nodded 'yes'. I remember we had a football match screws v cons and everyone was out to watch it and I played in goal for the cons. It was like a game of murder ball not football, our team was shit but when we scored the crowd went nuts it was good fun. We lost the game though and some of the tackles were horrendous.

I got a letter off my mam to say that my old boxing club the United Services were taking all the gear out of the gym as the building was to be demolished. It is now a car park in the town centre and I bet when the people are parking up they wouldn't know how much blood, sweat and tears had been spilled on that spot.

I saw the gym orderly knock a lad out cold with a hockey stick, hit him around the head and almost killed him, because he told everyone not to lift the stick above knee height and this lad did. I've seen big lads, heavily muscled, crying like babies in there. You had to be in and out the showers in quick time because Onslo the gym orderly would run in screaming 'Get Out' and bray anyone across the bare back or bare arse or legs with a hockey stick. He ruled by fear and intimidation and brutality.

Once a week was the dreaded 'Fence', a four mile run around the inside perimeter and there were some steep inclines which took everything out of your legs, it was hard and you had to do it in a certain time. Lots of people would spew up and others would cry in pain while the ones at the back got kicked, punched and dragged round. A few hours later we'd be put into teams and have to bunny hop up and down banks and have piggy back races and the more pain you were in, the more they enjoyed it.

I was walking up a corridor on my own and the screw called Bulldog was walking towards me, there was nobody else around and as he got closer he wouldn't even look at me so I bumped into him on purpose and he carried on walking and never said a word to me. What a shitty arse. When it was my time to leave the place I was glad to see the back of it.

I got my old flat back when I got out and had a weekend away with the lads at the lakes. It didn't end well as we were all pissed and the cops were called and one of the lads chinned a copper and we all got locked up. After about six hours we got let out on the condition we left town straight away or we'd get banged up so we headed home. My pal who punched the bizzie got remanded and when he went to court he got three years.

Not long after this I went to a Night Club and had been smoking a bit of blow and at the entrance I had an argument with one of the bouncers who looked like he lifted weights. I called him an idiot and he picked me up and threw me through the doors and out into the night. He followed me out and started to slam me off the walls, everything was in slow motion because of the blow I had smoked and I was lucky to land a punch on him and he went down. I just stood there looking at him as I was in a haze, the bouncer got up and brushed himself down and was mumbling something as he walked back into the club and closed the doors. I remember thinking I had been lucky to get away with that one because things could have been much worse.

Another night I had just came out of the Travellers Rest pub, I think I'd only had two pints, and was walking past three blokes sat on a wall over the road from the pub and one of them in particular, which happened to be the big one, was glaring at me as I got closer. I could see he'd had a drink and was looking for trouble so I said to him "Who are you looking at you fuckin' doyle" (doyle is a local slang word for idiot) and he was raging and shouted "Who are you calling a doyle" and jumped up and swung a big haymaker at me which I ducked under. I had one eye on him and the other on his two mates, so the big man threw a few shots at me and they all missed. His mates never moved off the wall and must have been waiting for him to chin me. When I realised they weren't going to get involved I focused on his because he was a powerful lad and he was trying to take my head off. I focused and moved in range and BANG, I landed a big right hand smack on the button and he went down like a sack of shit and was on the deck unconscious and not moving. The first thing that went through my head was I hoped I hadn't killed him, you hear stories like that all the time and it only takes one punch. His mates looked at me and never said a word. I was concerned for the big guy but didn't want to hang around in case the cops turned up so I jogged away from the scene. I turned around and saw them bent over him trying to bring him round. I was hoping he would be ok and I assumed he was when I never heard anything on the local news which was a relief. A few years later I saw him driving a council lorry doing the roads.

My friend Cliffy who I mentioned earlier got killed in a fight outside the night club, he was in the wrong place at the wrong time. There was an argument inside and someone got punched, then a phone call was made and a gang turned up armed with weapons and a big fight broke out. Cliffy who had nothing to do with the fight was accidentally hit with a baseball bat and staggered over the road, collapsed and died in the gutter. What a tragedy. There wasn't any CCTV in those days and the lad who got blamed for killing Cliffy was a friend of his and a friend of mine, there was no way it was him. He went to court and was found guilty and got a life sentence and after a few years it was overturned and he was released and rightly so. What happened to Cliffy was a tragic accident.

A few on us went to see U2 in concert, The Ramones were backing them as well as other bands like Spear of Destiny and what a great day we had but we almost never got there as the motor we were in conked out on the Motorway with a flat battery. We were up shit creek without a paddle but our luck was about to change when an Army convoy came in sight and at the front was an open top jeep with a Colonel in it. They pulled over and the convoy came to a halt. His name was Colonel Collins and he asked what the problem was and we said it was a flat battery so he ordered his boys to jump start it and in no time we were mobile again. We said goodbye and thanked the Colonel and his men and they drove off as we drove to the nearest garage and bought a new battery. Once the new battery was on it ran as sweet as a nut and we had no more problems with it. About an hour later we saw the Army convoy up ahead and as we went past it we tooted the horn and saluted the Colonel, who saluted us back with a smile on his face.

I had moved again and was living in a flat at Seaton Carew on The Green. I always like it at Seaton ever since I was a kid. When I moved in the people in the flat below thought a Rasta had moved in because all they could her was Reggae music. The beach was just over the road so I used to go running on it most mornings and after about a month I felt great so one Sunday morning I went down to the professional boxing gym to watch as I hadn't been in such a long time. In the ring was a Lt-Heavy shadow boxing, he was really fast and sharp and I hadn't seen him before but I knew he was very good just by watching him. He was warming up because he was going to spar, jackpot I thought, I'll watch a bit of sparring. To cut a long story short his sparring didn't turn up so me like an idiot said I'd spar and was gloved up and in the ring wearing jeans and shoes! After the first round I was gassed out but I did three rounds and the guy was trying to knock me out with every punch he threw! I took some heavy shots but I stayed on my feet. You would think after that I would have learned my lesson but years later I went to the Boys Welfare and the ABA Light-Welterweight champion Alan Temple was supposed to be sparring and his sparring never turned up. The professional boxing manager Gus Robinson was there and I saw how gutted Alan looked so I said I'd spar with him. So again I climbed through the ropes in a pair of jeans. I was under instructions to pull my punches but they need not have worried about that, he was too fast and I could hardly lay a glove on him but it gave him a bit of work. I would not recommend it to anyone who hasn't been in the gym for a while to just turn up and get in the ring and spar with any fighter let alone the ABA champion.

Fighting someone who thinks they can fight, like a brawler, tough guy, pub fighter, or whoever and fighting a boxer are two completely different things. The boxer is a trained fighter who knows how to judge distance, knows how to make you miss and capitalise on it, can think on his feet in the heat of battle, knows how to get the maximum effect from his shots, he knows where to place them and he's got good footwork and good balance and knows how to throw a punch correctly. You see a lot of so called tough guys having a fight and they throw wild haymakers and when they miss they fall over and look stupid, it's because they don't know how to punch correctly therefore they have no balance and hence, arse over tit they go. You can't learn it overnight it takes time, patience and practice to learn how to punch correctly.

ABA COCK UP

You know when some things happen in life and you think WTF happened there, well one of those times happened and I ended up in HMP Durham and it is hard to believe I got remanded for not taking video tapes back to the shop!

Believe me you couldn't make this shit up. My mate gave me his card for the video shop and asked me to pick some films out as I was passing that way, so I went and picked a few films out and gave him them and handed him his card back. The films didn't get taken back to the shop and they called the police because they had just installed a camera and the culprit was on video and hopefully could be identified. Well I was the one on camera and got took to the police station and charged with theft! I hit the roof with my friend but the tapes had gone and he didn't know where, probably nicked.

It just so happened I was moving on the day I was at court, so to speed things up so I could be in and out and get back for the move, I pleaded guilty. I was left in shock when the judge remanded me to HMP Durham for ten days. I couldn't believe it.

Durham was a shit hole and because I pleaded guilty I had convicted myself and had no privileges like other remand prisoners so I was on 23 hour bang up with no radio or anything just the four bare walls and an alcoholic, I had nothing in common with, for company. It was nice to get out once a day for an hour at a time for some fresh air on the exercise yard and those ten days felt like a month. It was embarrassing to tell people on the exercise yard that I was in for not taking video tapes back to the shop, do you know how ridiculous it sounds. I kept myself to myself and didn't want to get into trouble in there and get another charge, that wouldn't look good when I went back to court. The infamous prisoner Paul Sykes was in there at the time and I saw him a few times and knew who he was because of the boxing but I didn't befriend him. Once when we came off exercise and I was going to my cell, Paul Sykes was stood there on the landing eye-balling me but I just ignored him. My thoughts were on freedom not incarceration.

When I was back at court my solicitor was dumfounded why I was sent to prison for such a minor offence and I recall it was a different judge and he shook his head in disbelief, told me to pay the shop compensation of a certain amount and set me free. Looking back now it's still hard to believe it.

I got a job on Site Clearance which was pretty easy, we'd have to wait in the cabin for a phone call to go here or there and clear things up but the phone only rang a few times a week, the job was a doddle. We'd get paid on Friday's and everyone went to the bank for their wages and sometimes we'd go to the pub at lunch time and stay there but the Gaffer was ok and never used to say nothing as long as you didn't take the piss too much.

I went back to boxing but a different gym as my old one closed, and the building demolished, and by then my old trainer Duncan had passed away. These were a new set of lads and some were National champions and if you were present for a sparring session you were in for a treat because it was always heavy stuff. Every training session started with a run to warm everyone up and the coach Peter used to put everybody through their paces, he'd watch who was putting effort into it and who wasn't and woe betide if you weren't. I remember sparring and getting caught by an elbow and my eye brow spurting open so off I went to hospital and got more stitches. It's all part and parcel of the game.

I also used to play football at weekends for local pub teams always in goal of course as I was shit as an outfield player. I would never back out of a challenge. I was pretty physical and was always diving at people's feet. Once when I went for a 50-50 ball with the oppositions attacker and dived at his feet and won the ball, he screamed out in pain 'they've gone' and passed out. An ambulance was called and it came on the pitch and took him to Hospital, he had two broken legs and was in plaster up to his waist for months. It's a funny old game as some say but I enjoyed playing in goal and wasn't too bad actually and even had trials for Halifax Town FC but played shit and didn't impress. Boxing and Football I don't know where I got the energy from.

There was a boxing gym not far from me that I started training at and the coach was Tony who I'd known since we were kids. Tony was a good boxer himself as a youngster and contested five National finals. He had a couple of good lads in the gym and one of them was Andy Tucker who was a Young England International and Junior ABA Middleweight champion. I done a lot of sparring with Andy and he really was a cracking prospect with a big future ahead. I had a few fights for the club, all wins as you can imagine, but had outgrown the Light-Heavyweight division and was now a full blown Heavyweight.

A lad came to the gym for sparring, he'd had lots of fights on the circuit and kept asking Tony if he could come to the gym and spar with me so Tony said yes come along. I think he just wanted to test himself, or maybe test me, but he came straight at me full of beans and was letting the punches go with venom, I didn't think they were hurtful but they got my attention and he had a stinging jab, a bit like an angry bee. I hit him with a terrific body shot and he went down. He had a minute or so to recover his breath and said he wanted to continue so back at it we went and back at me he came all guns blazing. A few seconds later I sunk another rib tickler into him and he went down again only this time he didn't want anymore. Tony said to me "He won't be back to spar" and he was right. The lad never came back.

Tony worked as a bouncer in a pub called The Clarendon and asked if I fancied it so I went along and done the weekend to see if I liked it and it was ok, different but still ok. It was a really busy place with a disco upstairs. Sometimes four of us worked two up and two down, and the odd time five of us worked. I learned the ropes from the lads, how to control the queues and crowds, always be in control and never flustered, be firm but fair and be polite, good manners don't cost anything. We had a few fights but generally everything went fine and I had some good nights working with the lads.

Some of the lads off the door came to watch me fight this big guy at a boxing show. He was built like a brick shithouse and I could see the looks on people's faces when I told them I was fighting him I think they were concerned for my safety. On my walk to the ring I felt good and couldn't wait to get in there and fight, I was right up for it. He flew at from the opening bell and tried to put me away, he was hitting me with his big guns but I can take a shot and I was full of fight so I hit back and we traded blows while the crowd went crazy, he buckled first and I put him down. After an eight count the ref waved us to continue and I was all over him like custard over a jam roly-poly and he was just going down as the ref stopped it. It was exciting and the crowd loved it. The lads who came to watch were absolutely buzzing.

I stopped a lad from Sunderland in two rounds and it was all systems go. I was ready for an assault on the ABA Heavyweight title. When the day of the ABAs arrived I was excited like a kid in

73

a sweet shop, I'd been waiting for this and was confident I would do well. It was going to take a good man to beat me. I was fit, strong and sharp through all the sparring with Andy Tucker. We arrived at Gateshead Leisure Centre and I went to get weighed in but the official in charge said the weighing of boxers was over 10 minutes ago and he wouldn't let me get on the scales. A heated argument ensued and he still wouldn't let me get weighed, what a bell end. He said that every club had been sent a letter telling them that boxers had to be weighed in by 7pm. It was the first time we had heard of such a letter and were totally in the dark about it. He was adamant I wasn't getting on the scales and started to put them away. My ABA title dream died right there and I was gutted. We found out later that there was a letter but it was sent to the social club and not the coach as it should have been. The treasurer or whatever he was, of the social club read the letter and put it in a drawer and forgot to tell anyone about it, I could have smashed the blokes face in over it. My dream died because of him. All the hard work was to no avail. It's hard to describe how I felt but it wasn't nice. I was devastated. I believe I could have gone all the way or at least to the final stages. It done my plug in and I stopped going to the gym.

Four months later there was a knock at the front door late at night and when I opened it I was surprised to see Tony the boxing coach. I invited him in and wanted to know what he wanted. He said "You might think I'm crazy but I have to ask you. There is a boxing show tomorrow night in Blackpool and they are desperate for a Heavyweight, will you fight", Bloody hell I wasn't expecting that. I said "I haven't been in the gym for four months", "Howay man it'll be a night out in Blackpool" he said. I said I'd be the one taking the punches so I wouldn't exactly call it a night out. Maybe I have taken too many shots to the head but I said ok I'll fight and the next day we headed to Blackpool to a place called the Horse shoe. There were a lot of fights on and when they put the fight list up on the board and I saw I was the 16th fight. "16th we are going to be here all night". It was a big place and a capacity crowd and the place was hot and humid. The night dragged on and on and I was in the red hot dressing room trying my hardest to sleep but I couldn't, it was too hot and I was sweating like a pig. Around midnight possibly later I was told to get gloved up. I had no get up and go my energy was depleted. I tried to hit the pads but I had noting in me, no strength or power, I was sluggish and lethargic. I wanted a bed not a boxing ring. The heat had sapped all the strength out of me. A bloke came in and shouted 'You're on' and we made our way through the cloud of cigarette smoke to the ring and someone shouted 'TYSON' at me. My opponent was a local lad who had a lot of support. He was very tall maybe 6ft 4in or 6ft 5in and I tried to put him away early because I knew that was my only chance but my punches had nothing in them. It is moments like this when you are in the heat of battle and know you are going to have to dig deep to hear the final bell. I backed to the ropes quite a lot while he hit me with combinations of four, five and six punches but they had no effect as I slipped and covered up. I hurt him in the second round with a body shot but couldn't capitalise on it as I had nothing in the tank. In the third I summoned up everything I had to land a big uppercut but it just missed and that was my last throw if the dice. I was shattered and for the first time in my life I tried to get disqualified. I backed to the ropes and as he came after me I bounced off them and nutted him, I was hoping to cut him so the fight would be stopped but I got him in the middle of the forehead. I tried to make out it was an accident but it was a professional foul and the crowd were booing like mad and someone shouted 'Dirty Bastard', they knew it was no accident. The ref gave me a right ticking off for using my 'shoulder' and deducted a point, it was on his blind side and he was the only person in the place who never saw it properly. That gave me a bit of time and I made it to the final bell but lost the decision. I would have beaten him inside two rounds if I'd been in shape.

Boxing in Hartlepool has its roots in bare knuckle when people used to fight on the beach at Seaton Carew. In the early 1900s there was a boxing booth on the corner of Burbank Street known as the 'Blood Tub' which drew good crowds for people wanting to see punch ups. Hartlepool was a booming ship port in those days and the docks were thriving and teaming with people from all over the world. A man would go around the docks and pick five coloured seamen for an 'All In' at the Blood Tub. It was one man in each corner and one in the middle and when the bell rang it was everyman for himself, the winner was the last man standing. The 'All In' always drew a big crowd. During the depression people would fight for boxes of groceries or a couple of shillings, they were hungry fighters in them days.

Hartlepool's first boxing star was Jasper Carter, people today will never have heard of him but a hundred years ago he put our town on the fistic map. He won a few titles and most of his 300 fights were over 20 rounds. He was only a lightweight but he fought the Irish Middleweight champion Jack Lavery in front of 80,000 fans at Celtic Park in Belfast and stunned the crowd by knocking Lavery out in the first round. In his prime he was matched with the World champion 'Peerless' Jim Driscoll but the day before the big fight, Driscoll pulled out. Carter would say it was his biggest disappointment. He was introduced from the ring with former World Heavyweight champion James J. Jeffries and another time appeared in a boxing booth at Durham with the legendary Jem Mace. Carter was so confident that he could beat anybody his weight in Great Britain that he challenged any man

76

to meet him for £100 a side which was a lot of money a century ago. He was in the cinema watching a boxing film called 'The Set Up' when he became unwell and was taken to hospital where he died a few hours later aged 63. They don't make them like Jasper Carter anymore.

EUREKA MOMENT

I'm going to give you a short break from the Noble Art to tell you two little true stories about The Supernatural, if you don't want to read them and think it's all just a load of mumbo jumbo then just skip these two stories and resume again on another page.

I was doing a bit of security work with a lad called Stewie and he told me about this book he'd been reading called 'Voices in My Ear' about an old medium. It sounded really interesting so I went to the library and borrowed it. I read it and enjoyed it and was fascinated by some of the stories in it so when I took the book back I asked the receptionist if there were any mediums in the area. She had a look and said 'here's one' and gave me the number of a lady called Ruby Webster. I phoned her and she said she held a 'Philosophy Night' every Thursday and she invited me along. I was expecting messages from the dead not 'philosophy' so out of curiosity I went. I listened to her philosophy and her stories and really enjoyed myself so I started going regular. She would say 'if you are coming for messages you are coming to the wrong place'. Anyway I enjoyed going but I was questioning if there was an afterlife and wanted proof and the only way I was going to do that was to get my own proof. I decided to conduct a little experiment just to see if what she was preaching was true or bullshit, I don't like wasting my time listening to bullshit, no matter how good it may sound. I'm a realist not a fantasist. I said nothing to nobody about it and got a photo of my dad and for a couple of minutes each day I would talk to it, not out loud just in my head like I was talking to him as if he was stood in front of me. I told him about these philosophy nights I was going to and how I enjoyed them but I don't like to waste my time on rubbish if there is no truth in it. 'Please Dad I know if there was a way of you coming through and communicating with me I know you would. If you can hear my thoughts I'm asking you to give me a message to let me know I'm not wasting my time. If you don't then I know it is all bullshit'. I stayed away from Ruby's for a couple of weeks and decided this week I was going and it would be my last time. I spoke to my dad's photo every day in the build-up. You might think I'm crazy but this was my experiment, I was asking a question that I wanted answering and if no one could answer it, then I had my answer. Anyway the philosophy night at Ruby's went like all the rest and she had just called an end to the evening and I was sat there thinking 'I've enjoyed it here but I'm not coming back because in reality it's all a load of crap' but reality was just about to bite me on the arse. All of a sudden I seen Ruby nearly lose her balance and grab hold of something. She steadied herself and addressed everyone "I've got a man here he said his name is Tommy and he is here for someone", my god I knew it was my dad but I couldn't speak, couldn't even open my mouth. Ruby described the kidney dialysis machine and a few other things but I was sat there speechless when she was asking 'who knows this man' I could see her communicating with someone who was not visible to anyone else in the room, 'Someone here knows this man' she said and then she blew me away with what she said next "Someone here has a photo of this man and they talk to it with their mind". WTF, she blew it out the water with that one and I still couldn't open my mouth. It was such a realisation that my dad came through for me and my question was answered. It was a Eureka moment. It was 'my' Eureka moment. I was walking on air after that and I wrote Ruby a letter and told her the man that she had communicated with was my dad.

When I was 13 or 14 I slept at my Uncle Roy's and there were a few of us going to camp out in his garden but everyone changed their minds and went home but I stayed and slept on the couch. I don't know how long I'd been asleep, as the house was in darkness and everyone else was in bed asleep, but I was suddenly woken up! My face was facing the couch but whatever had woken me up was behind me and I knew there was something because I could feel like a vibrating current of energy, a bit like electricity. I tried to ignore it because I was too scared to turn around but it wouldn't go away and the hairs on my body were stood on end. I plucked up the courage to turn around and nothing could prepare me for what I saw. There was an old woman sat in the chair opposite me looking at me. I leapt off the couch like a scalded cat and ran upstairs in to Roy and Jean's room and woke them up. I was white with fear and now I know were the expression 'you look like you've just seen a ghost' comes from. I told Roy and Jean that I'd just seen the ghost of an old woman in the chair in the front room and she had woken me up. It sounded ludicrous but it was true. The look on my face should have told them all they needed to know and I said I wasn't going back down in the front room to sleep. Roy went down and had a look and found nothing but what was he expecting to find, If he walked in there in total darkness and she was still there he would have passed out. He came upstairs and said there was nothing there and it was my imagination. I know what I saw and it wasn't my imagination. I wasn't woken up by my imagination. It was a real ghost, a real spirit.

About 30 years after that happened I got in a taxi and the driver said "I can remember you when you were young you used to go to Roy's house. He lived over the road from my mother", I replied that Roy still lived in that house and had been there over 40 years. The taxi driver then said something that almost made the hairs on my neck stand up, "He was the second person to live in that house, before him an old woman lived there she was in her 70s and she was always shouting at the young kids who played outside, nobody liked her, she was known as the 'Old Witch'. I told him about what happened to me when I slept over that night and his eyes widened. He said "you saw her". All these years had gone since it happened and I know what I saw and nobody could tell me any different, another Eureka moment.

BOUNCER

After having a taste of working as a 'Bouncer' or 'Doorman' which ever you prefer, I like 'Bouncer' I think it is more old school I started working as a bouncer at The Clansman. I was confident enough and I had learned a bit from working at the last place and most of all, the most important thing about a bouncer in my day, I could fight. The landlord at the time was a former bouncer who knew the ropes and worked for many years on the doors and would give me the odd tip which I appreciated and took on board. He paid me a fantastic compliment when I heard he asked for me to work his doors because he knew they would be in good hands. Two of us looked after this boozer; there was a pool table and bar downstairs and a very busy weekend disco upstairs. I used to say to the people in the downstairs bar "Get yourselves upstairs there's a whole lot of shakin' going on."

Charlie was my work partner. I remember him from when I was a kid on the caravan site as he had relatives on there and had a reputation as a nutcase even then. He wore a steel plate around his stomach so that if anyone hit him there, they would bust their hand and you couldn't see it under his clothes but it was there. He had the credentials to be a doorman back then as he'd been to prison a few times for shoving guns down people's throats and things of that nature and was well known. You didn't need an interview with a CV like that, the job was yours. After work we would have a couple of drinks then go home. When groups of lads came in they were told in layman's terms to behave themselves or face the consequences. When you speak to them like that it will go one way or the other and most of them lose their bottle when they see you mean every word. Bouncers didn't mess about with the non-contact approach of today, any trouble and it was dealt with by violence. People would say don't cause trouble in that pub because so and so is on the door. The bouncer was a man of respect and demanded respect, that was the way it was back then and nobody had a license.

This bloke came in one night and had a massive bust up with his woman then he walked up to the bar and started smashing all the pint glasses that were stacked up waiting to be washed, he was obviously in a rage, I was walking back into the room when I heard the glasses smashing as Charlie was checking the downstairs bar. The bloke went to leave but had to walk past me to get through the door, the whole pub where watching and he was walking towards me with a snarl on his face. I stood in the way to block him and he threw a punch at me which I slipped and hit him with a straight right hand in the face and he was on the deck groaning and all the fight had gone out of him. Right at that moment Charlie arrived back and took the guy in the toilets to be cleaned up as his face was covered in blood, I had knocked some of his front teeth clean out and one had stuck in my hand, my knuckles were throbbing and pissing with claret. A few weeks later I got locked up over it, someone had put him wise about getting compensation but the CPS kicked it out. It's amazing how many arsehole like that bloke there is out there.

I worked at that place for a bit and songs like 'Pump up the Jam' remind me of my days there but my services where required elsewhere and I moved on to other establishments. I worked all the roughest bars in town, all the troubled spots, and went in to sort them out and bring a little order. Violence is the only language some people understand so I had to dish plenty of it out in order to create a more stable environment and stop the wannabe gangsters and hard men taking a hold and scaring the punters off. I worked with some good lads as well and some of them are no longer with us but there memories live on.

Every bank holiday in them days was an all-day session from 11am onwards, it was like a religion in those days. Bank Holiday was a massive drinking session for the whole town and people like me had to work the doors and keep the punters as safe as possible. People looking for trouble who came in the pub I was working, would soon find it because I would take no prisoners with these people.

I was working a pub just off Church Street one night and a hard man called George had a grievance with the man who ran the door team who I worked for. I was mainly freelance and worked for whoever I wanted but at this time I was on with these lads. This George could fight he was in his prime and about 17 stone. I had known of him as a hard man for a number of years. He was on a mission and was going round this night knocking the doormen out in each pub, that took some doing but he was doing it and he was heading in our direction. We got called to a pub near us that had our doormen on, there was fighting and they needed us, it was George but he had already left when we got there. We went in and the bouncers had been done over, shirts ripped off, teeth knocked out, claret and glass everywhere. I ran back to the pub I was looking after and arrived before he got there. There was a lot of anticipation in the air as around ten doormen had been assaulted and it was chucking out time when George suddenly appeared. Blackie who George was looking for was stood with me when George turned up and he started fighting with him immediately. He gave it his all but George started giving him a beating and I couldn't allow that to happen so I jumped in and pulled George off and threw him out the way. Lots of people were already in the street and plenty more were coming out the pubs, I knew this was it and I was ready when George said to me "I want to fight you" and motioned me to follow him into the road to do battle. We squared up and as he got close I hit him with a right uppercut and in a split second hit him with another and he was still stood there but I knew them shots would have taken everything out of his legs so before he got time to think, I landed a cluster of head shots and he went down. You know when someone is done and he was done so I walked back into the pub in case the coppers came by because they were always in the area. In the pub I heard an excited punter say to someone "Did you see Richy do him." George didn't take his beating very well and stabbed all the tyres of the cars in the street but, not long after, we settled our differences and became friends.

I was weighing sixteen stone by now and I was going boxing at the Boys Welfare again and sparring with the best lads they had, it was always a challenge up there and I had some good quality sparring. I was still growing and getting heavier and I remember something my mam said about when she took me to the doctors when I was a child and he told her "This child is going to be built like 'Man Mountain Benny' when he grows up." She said that to me a few times over the years and I used to laugh and thought it was a joke but a few years ago my wife Wendy googled 'Man Mountain Benny' and he wasn't a myth, he was an old time American wrestler and built like his title suggested. The doctor wasn't wrong as when I did 'grow up' I've always weighed around 20 stone.

I started going to a kick boxing gym as I was friends with the trainer. Every session started with a run and I would always trail in last. In the gym I noticed they were brilliant with their legs and feet but not so good with their hands, even the trainer didn't see it but I did, I had been around the fight game a long time. I suggested I get in the ring with them and spar just using hands no feet, the purpose of this was to bring them on with their punching and the coach was happy with that. I'll make a suggestion and if it's not acted upon it isn't my problem, it is free advice take it or leave it.

I'd get in the ring and spar with them and tell them they could hit me as hard as they wanted while I would pull my punches. I'd spar eight hard rounds straight off and they would say "How come you can do eight rounds like that, I'm fitter than you but I'm shattered after two". Like I've already said I had been around a while and it was down to one thing, Experience. The trainer took me for a couple sessions of kicking and wanted me to have a few kickboxing fights and then enter the British championships, he said I had what it takes to go all the way but all that kicking wasn't my cup of tea and I declined his offer.

I was bouncing with my mate Vulture in a new bar that had opened on the sea front it was a Karaoke bar with a night club at the back and up some stairs. It was packed out most nights and we'd shut the place at 11 and work the night club until 2am.

The Karaoke bar done my head in after a bit, I was sick of hearing the same songs over and over sang by people who couldn't sing a note but I did laugh my head off at a few of them as you can imagine. Even Vulture would get up now and again. He was actually one of the better ones and could do a good rendition of Holding Back the Years by Simply Red. One night there was a brawl with a couple of families god knows what it was over, maybe one was a better singer, they were the older generation so couldn't be dealt with in the normal way with a fist. One of them faked a heart attack and was laid on the floor. I knew he had faked it instinct told me that but the Ambulance had to be called and they turned up and put an oxygen mask on him and off he went and order was restored as the rest were ejected. We got word later that there was nothing wrong with the bloke who got took away in the Ambulance, he had faked the heart attack, maybe he just wanted to avoid the whole situation of the family fight and saw that as his only way out of it.

My pal Vulture got nine months in jail for an assault that happened a while before, so other doormen where brought in to work with me. I knew my time there was limited and soon I'd be on my travels to a new place.

The new place was a hive of activity in the town centre and the place to be it was jam packed all the time. It was two places in one. The downstairs had a pool table to the right of the front door and was usually packed five deep at the bar. At ten o'clock on weekend's it was the 'Ten o'clock Rock' and the place was constantly full to the brim. People loved the ten o'clock rock. Upstairs was just as big with a DJ and dance floor and that was always packed out. I knew once I started there I would be fighting all the time and it proved to be the case. There were a good team of doormen looking after the place and my first night they told me about this guy who was a bloody nightmare, he came in at weekends and would never see his drink off when asked and made them look stupid in the process because he loved an audience. I told them he'd be seeing his drink off tonight and to let me know who he was. It was late and there were only a few people left to get out, It was always a bit of a headache asking people to leave who were tanked up, anyway I noticed some lads pissing about stood round the doormen who were talking to this guy. Every time they asked him to see his drink off he would pick it up and wave at it to 'see it off'. It didn't take me long to realise it was the dickhead who would never drink up so I went over and took charge of the situation. I told him to drink up straight away or I'm taking his drink off him, I don't like people taking the piss like that so I was always firm with them. He just looked at me so

I picked his pint up and poured it over his head and then flattened him with a right hand. His mates were shocked and shouted that they didn't want any trouble and left taking their idiot friend with them who incidentally went to the hospital and had received a broken nose as well as a broken ego. He was actually thinking of pressing charges but decided not to and never tried his stupid antics again and that situation was nipped in the bud. That was the thing about working the doors you seemed to be in a no win situation because there were that many cry babies who ran to the police.

One night I had a fight right in the middle of the forty or so stairs that led to the upstairs disco, the lad knew me from when I was a kid and started being clever so we went at it. I was trying to get my footing right so I didn't go tumbling to the bottom but once I landed one on his jaw he went down and was laid across the stairs and I cracked a couple more into him. The other doormen shouted "Richy he's had enough" but I already knew that.

I was having a late drink with Vulture in a Church Street bar and he said "You see him over there (nodding in the direction of a known 'face') he was being clever in Eddie's boozer last week. He wouldn't pay for his drinks and wouldn't leave when asked. I'm going to knock him out". Eddie was publican friend of ours who was recently deceased so what the bloke done was disgusting and out of order. I said to Vulture "I'll knock him out" and as he and his pal were leaving I put a right hand on his chin and he was unconscious. An Ambulance was called and as they were taking him out, his mate who was another known 'face' came running in full of hell and shouted ,

"Come on then, fuckin' try and do it to me".

Bish, Bash, Bosh and he was covered in blood on the deck and had to go to Hospital to get patched up as well so both of them went in the same Ambulance.

I started seeing a woman who worked in the night club, I didn't know at the time but she was nothing but trouble. I will call her by the name of Tramp, as you can see I can't stand her. I never paid for a drink when I was in there and my pals hardly ever did either so that was the only good thing about it.

Anyway one time I was talking to Tramp and noticed a lad throwing his arms about and shouting something in a threatening manner but I couldn't hear him because of the noise. There were two of them, a big muscular one and the littler one who was doing all the shouting. It looked like he was shouting at me so I locked eyes with him and pointed to myself while mouthing 'are you talking to me' and he nodded 'yes' and shouted something else but I couldn't hear any of it. I didn't know why I was the subject of his verbal onslaught as I had never seen him or the big guy before. People like this can't be talked to so I wasn't going to mess about. I put my drink down and walked over and hit the mouthy one with a beautiful three punch combination, the first one was a powerful right followed by a left right all in one flowing movement bang, bang, bang, and he was unconscious before he hit the deck. I turned my attention to the big guy and he shot off like Usain Bolt but he didn't get far and I caught him with a right and he went down like a sack of spuds, I didn't catch him with it properly but it dropped him all the same and now he was scurrying under tables so I couldn't get at him and the doormen turned up. The mouthy one was still unconscious and the bouncers couldn't revive him, he was still out like a light when he was stretchered out the place by the paramedics. His jaw was broken in four or five places and got wired up and he had to drink through a straw for a while. I found out the big guy had been Tramp's boyfriend for a couple of years and when they saw me talking to her the littler one started working himself because he thought his mate could handle anything as he was the hardest bloke in their colliery town.

Another time I was at the bar getting a drink and this bloke was stood there trying to look like the hardest man in the world with a ciggie hanging at the side of his mouth. He takes a draw and looks at me snake eyed and points in my face "Don't I know you" he said. "I don't know but they call me Richy Horsley" I replied and hit him with a left hook. He was stood there staring into space and couldn't move, knocked out standing up. I spoke to him but didn't get a response as he was on another planet. It was another hospital visit and another broken jaw, only in two places this time.

One night I was working in another bar with Vulture and around 50 pissed up lads came in and they were all rowdy and being complete arseholes. We tried the friendly approach but they didn't want to know, they just wanted to cause mayhem and trouble was in the air. They were all from Middlesbrough. The manager was beside himself worrying so we got on the phone and got a posse of lads down and when they arrived we turned the music off and I addressed them all with the lads stood behind me "Right lads I'm gonna start taking your drinks away and you are all going to leave. Now it's your choice to kick off or fuck off. I repeated myself, kick off or fuck off". Now the odds were even they didn't fancy it much so we started taking their drinks away and they all left.

Another time in a different club we got a call and there was trouble upstairs and I was the first one on the scene to find one of our doormen Frankie, on top of a lad holding him down on the dance floor so he couldn't get away, and about five of the lad's mates were booting hell out of Frankie. I dropped the first lad as the others arrived on the scene and we gave them a hammering. Frankie said they were booting him for what seemed like a minute and he kept sneaking a peak saying to himself, 'the lads will be almost here' but the idiot of a DJ didn't put the call over the system so we didn't know it was happening until someone ran in and told us. Frankie's health was at risk on that floor and things have a habit of taking a turn for the worst but luckily he was alright. I had some choice words for the DJ at the end of the night and he filled up with tears and packed in working there.

THE CAVEMAN

It was New Year's Eve and I had been working the door since 12 noon so by the time the Midnight chimes rang out you could say I was a bit tired and a little worse for wear. I'd had a few fights and a few drinks in those 12 hours and rather than call it a day I went to a couple of different house parties. It was about four in the morning and I went to the toilet and there was a lot of commotion on the landing because a lad was trying to get into the bedroom were a young girl was asleep, so I gave him a clip and staggered into the toilet while he was escorted downstairs. I could hear a lot of shouting as all hell was breaking loose downstairs and it was the lad's friend going mad, shouting he wanted to fight me in the garden. The guy who was shouting the odds was none other than Brian Suckling who had a fearsome reputation and would fight two or three people at a time if need be. He was as strong as a bull and had a punch that could demolish a wall. He had no fear and beat many hard men on his way up the ladder. Nobody wanted to fight this monster and he was also given the nickname The Caveman. I didn't want to fight him because I was pissed and very tired, but as he was outside screaming for me to join him on the grass to fight I felt like I had to go out. That was a stupid mistake on my part. I went into the garden and he hit me with a punch that almost took my head off and I hit the deck like I'd been shot, my legs were like jelly and I didn't know where I was but as I'm laid there, the man they call the caveman, didn't walk away, he got on top of me and started letting the punches go and they smashed into my face with sickening thuds. I couldn't lift my arms up to protect myself I was totally at his mercy. Nobody tried to drag him off because they were all terrified of him. While I was getting beaten to within an inch of my life, the lad who started all this shit kicked me in the head a few times. Brian Suckling kept smashing away and I thought he was trying to kill me because I could feel myself slipping away with every punch, I have a strong mind and kept telling myself to stay with it he'll stop soon, but it felt like an eternity to me before he stopped. The only reason he stopped was because he thought I was dead and I almost was. I was cut to ribbons, the flesh on the bridge of my nose was cut and both eyes were cut above and below. I was an absolute mess and the next day when the bruising started to come out I looked like I'd survived being hit by a train. I couldn't see out of one eye so I went to the eye infirmary and they said the eyeball was grazed but would heal.

The news of the 'fight' broke all over town and how easy I got beat. Brian was the new king on the throne and he revelled in it and told people time after time about how he beat Richy Horsley. It was all free drinks, hand-shakes and celebrity status for the new king. I was told he was going round like he was King Kong.

I stopped working the doors until I healed up and that took a while because I was in such a state. My pride was hurt and I was embarrassed by it all so I just kept a low profile and healed. Every day that night went through my head and all I could think about was the beating I took it was a horrendous beating and people have died for taking a lot less. I knew when I had healed and got my mind focused I wanted a return fight with the caveman, the new king. I don't really know how long it took before I was ready, maybe six months, I didn't train in the gym at all I just did a little shadow boxing in front of the mirror.

One night I got a phone call saying the lad who caused all the trouble was in the night club so I went down there immediately. I was stood through a set of doors at the back of the club while the doormen went to see him and told him they wanted a word with him because they believed he had been smoking weed. The door opened and he walked through and the bouncer shut the door behind him. I had a pint in my hand and dropped it as I went for him and slipped in it and as I fell I grabbed him and we both went tumbling down the stairs. It didn't start off as I planned, but I soon rectified the situation and started giving him it to head and body and he squealed like a pig. I left him outside the fire doors at the back of the club laid in a heap. I was glad to get hold of that wanker, one down one to go. Next would be the return fight I'd been waiting for with the new king, and about a month later I knew it was Judgement day. I wanted to know was it the drink or was he the better fighter, I had to find out and this time I wouldn't be drunk and tired I'd be fresh and a different fighter. We all know the risks, you live by the sword you can die by it but that's the code and I was prepared to fight to the death.

I took four lads with me to watch my back because he would have a posse with him so we went to the club where I knew he would be and sure enough, when I looked through the window, the big bastard was in there with his back to me. I banged on the window and everyone turned round and looked, I motioned to Brian to come outside, he knew what was about to go down. I walked over the road to give myself some distance for when he came out. He came out the door full of confidence and shouted "So you want another good hiding do ye" and came at me and threw a big right, the same one that done me last time, but I was ready for it and blocked it and put a couple of big shots on his chin and he went down. I got on top of him like he did to me, and smashed him to bits and broke both my hands. He was making funny gurgling noises when I got off him and I thought he was going to be brown bread. He was rushed to Hospital and luckily he pulled through but it was touch and go. I was back on top, Number 1. My pride was restored and people started to call me Crazy Horse because of my interest in the American Indian and because my name was

Horsley so the name Crazy Horse was appropriate and seemed to stick.

That fight reminded me a little of the fight I had when I was nine when I met someone at the swimming baths to fight. I took him at face value and turned my back to walk away and get a few meters room before we got it on but I had broken the rule of 'never turn your back on your opponent' and he jumped on my back and started to choke me. Luckily I managed to get him off and threw him down and smashed about ten punches into his head and it was all over. I had learned from it and that's why I walked over the road waiting for Brian so I had a bit of distance.

Word spread like wild fire about me and people where coming from all over to have a go and I was fighting a couple of times per week. I got locked up a few times but always had witnesses so was never charged. One Sunday I had promised myself a quiet night and trouble free, I had been working the pubs and clubs during the week and had a few fights so I went out to some bars and was in a chill out mood with a no trouble tonight policy on my mind. I went in a pub and got between two guys at the bar and one of them said "Who the fuck you pushing. Do you want chew" (chew is trouble). I bit my tongue and ignored him. "You better not if you know what's good for you" he said. I got my drink and went to the other side of the room and this prick was looking over at me and saying something to his mates. I thought to myself 'the quiet night is out the window'. When they went to leave I stood in front of the door blocking it, "I do want chew" I said and lifted the mouthy twat out his boots with a big right and he was sleeping on the floor with blood gushing from a deep gash. His two mates shit themselves and a woman was screaming her head off and the manager came over and told me to leave before the Ambulance and cops turned up.

Months after this I went to a pub to sort some trouble out but the lad I wanted to see had already left but who was sat there with all his mates but the mouthy guy who I chinned not long before. I didn't know this guy but when I made enquiries about him I was told he was a good fighter. Anyway I left the place and was walking to the car when I heard "Oi you" and when I turned round it was him with a load of lads behind him, a case of safety in numbers. He shouted "Who do you think you are. Don't ever come here to sort chew out in my pub", I ignored him because there was too many of them.

I drove to my mates boozer and got a few lads together and we went straight back over and when we went in the guy was on his own as all is so called pals had left the pub, they obviously knew I would be back. I offered him outside but he said no because he reckoned some of the lads would put the boot in to him. He wouldn't come out in the car park to fight me, not even just the two of us, but as soon as he started to raise his voice I thought I'd get into him and hit him a few times and he folded. I broke three of his ribs with a body punch and he had internal bleeding and was in a bad way. He paid an underworld hard man two grand to sort me out. The muscle was coming down to a certain place at a certain time so I went there with a few lads and had a pint and was told the twenty stone Bull Elephant was in the other room but I decided to drink my pint first. The head bouncer came over and pleaded with me not to fight in there but I told him to piss off and he walked away with his tail between his legs. I finished my drink and went in the other room and someone said "He's just left. He bottled it at the last minute." A while later I saw this hired muscle in the night club and stood directly in front of him eye-balling him, he shook his head at me to say 'no' and turned his back on me. You didn't get much for two grand.

The Tramp from the night club had started with the trouble causing again saying stuff about a local hard man called Davo Halse, who was supposed to be saying stuff like "Richy is fuck all", "Richy can't do nowt with me", "I would beat him easy", "I'll tie him in knots" and all the rest of it. I had known of Davo for many years, everyone knew him. He was a fighting man and a ladies' man. The women liked him because he was a bit flash and he was good looking, plus he had the patter. He was a character. I remember a bloke in our town, a fighting man who thought he was the hardest man since Superman until he came up against Davo and took a pasting. They had a return fight and Davo gave him another pasting. Believe me Davo could fight and as far as I knew he hadn't been beat so I wasn't taking this lightly and gave it some serious consideration. I decided I would take action and knew where he and his mates would be on Saturday afternoon so I went down there with two of my pals to watch my back. I waited at the bar and saw one of his mates come in so I knew he wouldn't be far behind, about six of them walked in before Davo came in last of all. I walked straight over and he knew what I was coming for so I threw a right hand and he tried to slip it but it caught him and he hit the deck with claret oozing from a cut. I bent over and hit him with a peach of a hook on the side of the jaw and his eyes rolled and he went out like a light. He lost a few teeth and wet himself. I said to his mates "come on then who wants it" but none of them wanted to know and wouldn't even look me in the eye. I walked out the back doors jumped in a motor and was gone. Only then did one of them pull a knife out and say 'he's getting this' and then the Ambulance came and took Davo away.

I knew how Davo was feeling because I had felt exactly the same after getting smashed to bits and humiliated off the caveman, your pride takes a hammering as well, but after this there were a lot of lies going around, things like I hit him from behind and stupid things like that. Another one was that I ran out the back doors and went straight to the police station demanding protection. I mean what sad bastard makes these things up. A lot of people believed it because to some people Davo was unbeatable and their hero, a bit like a boxing fan would look on Sugar Ray Leonard.

While Davo was licking his wounds life went on. I knew he would be back for another fight when the time was right.

One night in the club a bloke who used to run a bouncing firm who was a pal of Davo's came to where I was drinking and hovered about. He was being a total arsehole and I did my best to ignore him. He was on his own so I let the cheeky twat think he got one over on me. The next week he was there again and still being a bell end, obviously thinking he was the one who would get revenge and take my scalp back like a conquering hero, he thought he was a right handful. I was thinking 'I've had enough of this', he was a big man all twenty plus stones of him but more like a barrel and as soon as it went a bit quiet I shouted to him "Oi fat cunt you are getting on my tits", he came straight for me with a snarl on his face and wanted blood, he got blood but it was his own. As soon as he got near me I hit him with a right hand left hook and when they landed I knew I had broken both my hands, his huge head was like hitting a brick wall. He went down with a thud on the tiled floor in front of the downstairs bar and landed on his knees, and both knees broke because of his weight, my hands were in pain but I kept punching and knocked him out. The doormen wouldn't come near me but the manageress of the club was on my back screaming at me trying to pull me off him. She said she thought she had a death on her hands. He went to Hospital with two broken knees and a broken jaw and got stitched up like a road map. He brought it all on himself, he wanted it not me, he came looking for it and got it.

I laughed when I got told there were more lies flying around and I could hardly believe what he told people. He said I was with two lads and one was a Kung Fu expert. The Kung Fu expert swept his legs from under him, the other lad smashed his legs with an iron bar and I finished him off. What a fairy-tale he came up with. Anyone present would tell you a completely different story. I find it hard to understand why people can't tell the truth and you know what? Some people actually believed it. He was well connected and told this bullshit story to the Newcastle hard man Viv Graham and he was paying Viv money to sort me out. Rumours were flying around that Viv Graham was coming down to fight me because he was getting paid this amount and that amount and I would say 'well I'm not a hard man to find I'll be on the doors.' I knew a fight with Viv would be a hard fight but I certainly wouldn't be running scared I would stand my ground and fight. I was confident in my ability. I got a phone call off a guy I knew who said Viv Graham had just phoned him asking about me, I knew this to be true because he was friends with Viv so I asked what the conversation was about. He said "I told him you didn't take liberties and that you are a solid bloke and wouldn't do shit like they said you did." Viv said he had a feeling something wasn't true about the story and decided to leave it be. It was a nice touch for someone like Viv Graham to make an enquiry like that about me instead of acting on false information and it showed to me that the man had brains. There are always two sides to every story.

Another of Davo's pals came in the club and started being a cocky twat, it was like he was sending them in but I think they came in off their own back hoping to be the one who would get revenge. I walked over to him and put the nut on him, he was about 6ft 4in so I ended up catching him in the teeth and I had a cut on my forehead, I landed the big guns and he was another Hospital casualty and apparently in a right mess. Many years later I was talking to him and mentioned it and asked if it was about Davo and he said yes it was.

Some blokes had a meeting and wanted Davo present and they put forward a plan to have me shot and give Davo an alibi but he said he didn't want anything to do with it and he would sort his trouble out with me himself. Fair play to him, I respected him for that, a man of honour.

I heard reports he was looking really good and had been training for a while. I knew the fight wouldn't be too far off. I was at the club and two dykes came up to me and said "you're fighting Davo again soon eh aren't you scared", "Am I fuck he's the one whose getting knocked out" I said and they looked at me in disbelief. Some people actually had bets with each other on the outcome.

One Saturday afternoon the phone rang and it was Davo and he was ready to fight. I told him I'd been up all night and to phone me at tea time and we'd sort something out. When he phoned back we arranged to meet at 7 o'clock in the Owton Lodge car park.

He was wearing a white vest and looked in good shape, we showed each other respect and shook hands and he said

"It was a bit too fast last time. I've got to fight you to see who the better man is"

I nodded and smiled and knew exactly what he meant. Only a fighter would know that. We stood with our hands up ready for action and I threw out a light jab and he came under it like lightening and grabbed me round the waist and took me to the floor. We landed with a thud on the gravel and were both grappling to get the upper hand and I got on top of him. I grabbed his head and tried to smash it off the floor but his neck muscles were too strong and he hissed through gritted teeth "you dirty bastard" then I hit him with four big shots and it was all over. I stood up and there were little stones in my hands off the gravelled car park and as I walked away Davo said "Richy you can't leave me here like this", he couldn't stand up. He was a fallen warrior who went down fighting and that is something to be proud about in my eyes. I helped him get up and walked him to his car. The much talked about and anticipated rematch was over. I will say something about Davo Halse, he was a man of honour and I respect him for that.

A few of us went out round the town for a good drink to celebrate Vutlure's birthday and when we walked into a wine bar called Butler's, I saw the caveman Brian Suckling stood at the bar behind a post, he was with his wife and another couple. I didn't tell anybody I saw him because no one mentioned it so they can't have seen him. I knew they had seen me they couldn't have missed me, but I was thinking that the trouble with him was over and that he wouldn't start tonight anyway because he was with his wife and another couple and it looked like they were having a quiet night. I was aware he was there and then I watched them leave. After we'd finished our drinks and made our way out Vulture was talking to the doormen, I should have been more observant but as soon as I got out the doors and on to the pavement BANG my head exploded, at least that's what it felt like, a bit like a hand grenade going off in your head. There was a blinding flash before my eyes and then complete darkness and for a few seconds I didn't know where I was or what had happened. It was the caveman, he had hid and waited and as soon as I walked out the doors, he hit me with a massive right hand on the button and I flew back against the windows of the wine bar and he hit me with a couple more head shots and one of my mates jumped in and pushed him away to stop him attacking me further and while this was going on, I started to focus and realise what the hell had happened. Brian shouts "Come on then I'll fight the fuckin' lot of ye" and one of my other pals says "let them fight" and they clear a space and Brian moved back a little. I was back to my senses by then after being totally caught off guard, he'd hit me with his best shots and I took them and was still on my feet. I walked towards him with legs like jelly after absorbing them massive punches and my lips were cut and bleeding. There was a wine bar over the road called Oscar's with a huge glass front and everyone was up against the window's watching the remainder. We were in the main street that runs through the centre of town called York Road and cars were stopping because they couldn't get passed as Crazy Horse and The Caveman went toe to toe. This was the third fight, the decider, the grudge match. We are both stood trading shots, some miss and some land but the one that pulled it out the bag was a big left hook that landed on Brian's chin. When it landed I broke my hand and broke his jaw. What a punch and his eyes rolled in his head as he went down, it reminded me of the Sugar Ray Leonard-Dave Boy Green knockout. I dragged him off the road and got on top of him and give him some more, I couldn't get the image of that first fight out of my head, that's the reason why I did that and another reason is you don't let a man like Brian Suckling get back up because if you do he will kill you. Luckily an Ambulance was on the scene within a minute and got the oxygen mask on him and headed straight for Hospital and I thought he was going to die. He was in a very bad way in Hospital but somehow he pulled through, thank god. That's the fighting spirit in him. If I see him these days we'll wave or have a little chat, it's all water under the bridge now as we are in our 50s but our trilogy of brutal fights in the 1990s have passed into Hartlepool Folklore.

TIME FOR CHANGE

I was working for a cable firm as a cable puller but there was hardly any local work as it was all over the country. You could be at the very top of Scotland one week and in London the week after but that's life as a cable puller you travel all over the country and live out of your travel bag. I was doing it for a few months and the job what we were on came to an end and instead of waiting to be put on another job I went to graft with an old mate called Mick Sorby. I always got on well with him and I regarded him as a good friend and a top bloke. When anyone came into pubs and saw us working the door they would think twice about starting trouble. Mick had a sidekick called Peter who I'd known since I was young. He got a baseball batting round the head one night and was never the same after it. Peter was normally a lovely bloke who wouldn't do anybody a bad turn but since the baseball batting he started acting a little strange and getting on peoples nerves a bit which was totally out of character for him.

I had filled out a bit more and was now weighing in at 18 stone and living up to the prophecy the doctor told my mam when I was a small child that when I grew up I'd be built like 'Man Mountain Benny'.

As well as working the doors Mick and I done lots of other jobs like, a bit of debt collecting here and there, security, breaking jaws, taxing drug dealers and things of that nature. People who needed things taken care of or things looking after would contact us. The drug dealers were only scum bags anyway so it made no difference to anybody. We weren't doing any harm to the ordinary law abiding citizen, it was the bad people, the druggies, the low life horrible people who you read bad things about in the papers.

On the town one night with Mick and Peter we went into a club and ordered drinks and I said I'll be two minutes because I needed the toilet and went upstairs to the men's room. There was a Skinhead in there looking the worse for wear. Peter walked in and watched the proceedings as the Skinhead said to me "What's your name", so I told him and he perked up and his chest came out another six inches and he put his hand out for me to shake it. I went to shake his hand and he pulled his away and said "Dry your fuckin' hand first", what a cheeky bastard so I put a left hook on his chin and as he went down he banged his head off the piss pot and was laid in a pool of blood. He recovered and was ok.

Jobs were coming in all the time.

'Will you break so and so's jaw for a grand, 'Will you beat this one or that one up for this or that amount', it was easy money. One funny job I remember was I went to see a drug dealer because someone wanted him slapping about and I said to Mick 'wait here I won't be long' and he heard a commotion so after a few minutes he came to investigate. He said saw me having a word with the dealer who was dazed and in a sitting position with blood streaming down his face from a cut eye, and a plant pot on top of his head with the soil all over his shoulders. He couldn't get that picture out his head and it made him laugh for a long time. It was nothing personal it was just money and then on to the next job. That's the way it was and we had a good time along the way.

Mick was bad this weekend so decided to stay home and his sidekick Peter came to work the doors with me. Peter had worked on fishing boats all his life and he told some of his cod head pals to come and have a drink with him while he was 'bouncing'. When they turned up it was almost closing time and the place was practically empty and one of them was a huge guy who was built like a brick shithouse. They were pissed and started fooling around so I jokingly said 'put that big bloke out Peter' and the big man took it the wrong way and started shouting and getting aggressive. He wanted to fight me but when he put his hands up, his legs buckled and he staggered. I could have destroyed him but I don't take liberties and said I wouldn't fight him because he was drunk. I had visions of killing him if I hit him while he was in that drunken state. After he calmed down we agreed to fight the next week in the alley at the back of the pub 'Churchills'. After he sobered up he obviously had second thoughts and Peter came to see me during the week and said the big fisherman didn't want to fight me and has apologised and is very sorry for the way he carried on last week. He asked if it was ok for him to come in and buy me a pint and apologise in person, I said yes it is and that's what happened. He came in looking a bit sheepish and apologised, bought me a pint and left. Don't you just love a happy ending.

It almost wasn't a happy end when a friend of mine came was on home leave and his bird was seeing someone behind his back. We were having a drink and two blokes were getting a bit funny with him in the bar and one of them happened to be his bird's fancy man what he didn't know about or it would have cracked him up. One of my pals had a worrying look on his face so I asked what the matter was and he said our friend had a knife and was going to knife the two blokes. I knew it would be serious because he was on home leave for stabbings, I hadn't known the guy that long as he was already in prison, so with them being in my company I decided to put an end to it and knocked the two blokes out, one punch each. We left the pub and it saved them blokes from getting stabbed off the guy who I later learned to be a raving lunatic who stabbed lots of people. I hate knives and knife crime people should learn how to fight properly.

Another lad called Harry I'd known of since I was young, I became friends with him in the 90s and we'd socialise. He was another lunatic but I moved in them circles back then. He would just turn up in Churchills out of the blue and have a few drinks with Mick and I he was a gun for hire and lived life on the edge. He shot his father three times and then turned the gun on himself and blew his own brains out. I couldn't imagine doing that. His mind must have been in a bad place at the time for him to do something like that. It was Harry I went to for advice when I beat a connected drug dealer up. The dealer threatened to have me shot. Harry told me to take it serious because the dealer hadn't had anything like that done to him before and would be embarrassed so would have to do something about it. It was Harry's brother who made enquiries and there was a hit ordered but it hadn't been carried out but was in the process and it thankfully got stopped. Thanks Harry rest in peace.

I almost did get shot once, well twice actually, the first time I was in a lock in with Mick Sorby and the armed police came in and wanted our names. A few days later I found out why. It was because they had a phone call saying that someone was lying in wait with a gun and were going to shoot me when I left the lock in. The armed response acted on the tip and found the lad lying in wait like the informant said. Whoever knew it was happening must have had a conscience and probably didn't want it on their conscience if it turned out to be fatal. The other time was when a few of us went to watch a bare knuckle fight, at least that's what we were told and we only went to help a friend and give him a little back-up but when we turned up people pulled guns out and started shooting at us. The bullets whizzed by my head and started putting the van windows out. We jumped back in and off we went but one of the lads had two bullets in him and had to be dropped off at the Hospital. No more doing favours for people I said to myself.

There were quite a few of us having a night out and it was great to chill out instead of working the doors. There was a lad with us who was an ex-boxer who hadn't been out of prison very long after doing a stretch for armed robbery. I remembered him from my old gym. He was short and squat but strong but he thought he was a right hard case. I don't know how he ended up with our crowd but he did and the more drink he got down him the louder he became and he started to get on a few peoples nerves. We ended up in Churchills and out of the blue he shouted to me "Oi you outside me and you, I'm the best fourteen stone you'll come across", I thought he was joking but when I realised he wasn't I took my coat off and headed for the doors and someone shouted "Do him Richy".

Churchills had a big glass front so you could see outside and everybody was about to see how I fared with the 'best fourteen stone I'll come across'.

He came straight at me and I caught him on the chin with a short and powerful hook and he went down so I bent over him and put a few right hands on his jaw and he was on another planet. He was still unconscious when the Ambulance turned up and he was stretchered away with an oxygen mask on. They had to put a steel plate in his jaw as it was broken in four places. He brought it all on with his loud mouth and should never have offered me outside.

I called in a club to see my old sparring partner Andy Tucker who was working the doors, it was good to have a catch up with him I always had time for Andy, but while we were talking at the bar a lad comes over and stands in front of me in a boxing stance and starts flicking jabs in my face! I told him to behave himself and go away as I was talking. I warned him and he took no notice. He should have walked away then and everything would have been hunky dory but he didn't go. I had a quick scan of the place and a lot of people were looking so I started to feel a little embarrassed because he was still flicking out the jab, I put my drink on the bar and flattened the guy. I apologised to Andy and left the club. A few weeks later the guy's brother who was a boxing coach said to me "what did you do that to our kid for", I told him what happened and he was told something completely different. He said his brother's jaw was broken in two places and was wired up.

Back at the boozer but on a different day, there was a group of lads who used to frequent it and one of them was a stocky lad with a skinhead who a friend of mine said was an up and coming fighter and would soon be a name in the town. My friend said the lad had beaten some good fighters and was well respected by his age group of early to mid-twenties.

It was bank holiday and there was trouble in the pub so Mick and I flew over to sort it out and one of their crown was fighting so I got hold of him to throw him out and the stocky lad grabbed my arm and told me to "leave him", I said "He's going out and if you don't shut your mouth you are going out with him", and he replied "I'm not".

I passed Mick the lad who I was putting out and asked him to escort him out while I turned my attention to the stocky lad who was challenging my authority. I didn't say anything else to him I just hit him with a cracking right hand and he hit the deck. It looked like he was trying to get up and I wanted to keep him down so I kicked him in the head and there were gasps from people but he wasn't getting back up and was laid flat out. His mates carried him outside and when the Ambulance arrived, the paramedics worked on him because he had almost swallowed his tongue. Thankfully they managed to bring him round and after about thirty minutes they left. The cops were there and told the lad they know who did it and wanted him to grass me up but he wouldn't. They were looking over at me and I thought I was getting arrested but the lad wouldn't say anything and didn't want to press charges. I was thinking that if I stayed working the doors, sooner or later I would end up in prison so I was giving it serious consideration about packing it in. The door supervisors badge was coming out and everyone had to be registered so old school doormen like me wouldn't be allowed on the doors. I had done my time as a bouncer and it was time for change.

I went back cable pulling and was all over the country again in a cable gang. There is always plenty of work on the cable gangs and it can be very hard work but it gives you a bit of money in your pocket and keeps you off the dole, but you have to be willing to work hard.

During a weekend home it was my birthday and a few of us went out for a drink. I will tell you this story as I was told it because I have no recollection of any of it. I was drinking whiskey straight and also pints but mainly whiskey and was drunk in a few hours. We went from pub to pub and I was putting the whiskey away like it was going out of fashion. One of the lads who went out drinking with us was an old friend who was also called Richy and he had caused some trouble with some lads who were enjoying themselves on the dance floor. He decided he was getting tore into them and fighting broke out. Richy was terrible when he had a drink, it was like he had a chemical reaction and it sent him violent. I on the other hand am not like that when I've had a drink.

Everywhere we went these same lads seemed to be in the same pubs and Richy was always straight over fighting with them. Not nice behaviour for someone out celebrating your birthday with you. Now I don't know about you but if I was out on somebody's birthday the last thing I would want to do is fight because it spoils the night. If I was sober I would guarantee there would have been no trouble because I would have nipped it straight in the bud but, because I was so drunk I was oblivious to it.

These lads were from out of town and there were about thirty of them scattered about in different pubs and as the end of the night approached I was propping the bar up by myself as everyone had gone elsewhere and I didn't want to go so I just stayed where I was. I am relaying this story to you as I was told it by various people and I pieced it together.

In the meantime the lads from out of town had all met up and were enraged at the trouble this Richy had been causing so they all headed down to his last known location, all 30 of them, it was around 1-45am when they arrived, but the doormen wouldn't let them in because they knew there was going to be trouble and the place would get smashed up. They were asking for Richy.

The famous bare knuckle fighter Bartley Gorman was once told 'they will come for you when you are drunk Bartley', that was certainly the case with me, 'they will come for you when you are drunk Richy' even if it was the wrong Richy they wanted, I think anybody would have done they just wanted blood. A lad was talking to me at the bar at this same time and he later said he could hardly understand anything I was saying because I was slurring so much. He said a bouncer came over and said "Richy there's about 30 lads outside want you and are looking for trouble", the lad walked over to the bay window what gave you a view of the street outside and he saw all the lads, most of them were tooled up with empty beer bottles in their hands and he came back over and said "Richy don't go down there or you'll be killed" and he said I slurred something like "I'll have some of this".

He said I got up and staggered to the stairs and made my way down to what looked like my death, so he went over to the bay window to see what happened. Hey I didn't care, I was a gladiator. Live by the sword, die by the sword.

He watched me stagger outside into the street and get attacked immediately with punches, kicks and bottles over the head. I was fighting on memory and started landing punches and dropping them. The lad at the bay window said he couldn't believe what he was watching. The bouncers were stood watching the action open mouthed. I had a go but there was far too many and they were coming behind me and smashing bottles over my head and I started taking a beating and went down and got kicked unconscious.

I was told I put seven of them in hospital but the lad watching from the bay window said he counted nine. So all in all I gave a good account of myself considering the circumstances. I remember waking up the next morning and looking at the ceiling thinking something wasn't right, so as my eyes began to focus I realised I was in Hospital and didn't have a clue what I was doing there. As I sat up, the pillow was stuck to my head with dry blood and the room was spinning as I had the mother of all hangovers. I shouted for a nurse and asked what I was doing in Hospital and she said I was admitted with head injuries and the doctor wanted to see me this morning and if I hadn't been so drunk I would have died. She asked if I wanted any breakfast and I said yes so when she went to get me some, I quickly put my clothes on and left.

I didn't have a clue what happened until I started asking people and that's how I pieced it together. They were lucky I wasn't sober! I don't bare any grudges, shit happens. It might have been a bit of karma after all the punishment I had dished out.

NOBLE ART

I went to a boxing show with lots of old friends from the boxing world to see a friend fight over six rounds and the American Heavyweight puncher from the 70s Ernie Shavers was the guest of honour. It was a great night and good to catch up with the boxing lads, one of which was Graham who was head coach at the Boys Welfare Amateur Boxing Club. He invited me over to watch the lads train and spar so I went over a few times and while I watched I was soaking up the atmosphere and it was getting in my bones again so I started to help out. Once a year there was a coaching course and Graham asked if I wanted to go on it and get my coaching badge as the course was coming up in three weeks and one of the lads called Neil Fannan was going on it, so we could go together and the club could have three qualified coaches.

It was an intense course over four full days, over two weekends, and on the first day I was sweating buckets as I hadn't done any training for a long time. One of the instructors said to me "you should leave the beer alone before you come here" but I hadn't had any I was just unfit and sweating like a pig. Neil Fannan was my partner throughout the four days, and when we were going through various blocks and combinations, I would slip a hard one in when he wasn't expecting it and he'd look at me and his eyes would say 'you crafty bastard'. Then when I'd forgotten about it and relaxed a bit, Bang, I would get the same treatment and he'd have a grin like a Cheshire cat. I will put the course down here because it might be of interest to some people. Things might have changed a little because it was 20 years ago but they won't have changed that much.

PART ONE - SATURDAY

9-15 Course assembles. Review of programme. ABA coaching scheme. Examination procedure.

9-30 Basic Skills (practical)

10-45 Break

11-15 Roll of the coach

12-15 Basic Skills (practical)

1-00 Lunch

2-15 The sport of amateur boxing

3-00 The ABA club

3-45 Break

4-15 Basic Skills (practical)

5-30 Equipment essential for club and boxer

6-15 Close

PART ONE - SUNDAY

9-15 Course assembles

9-30 Basic Skills (practical)

10-45 Break

11-45 Coaching boxing skills

12-00 General first aid (Theory/Practical)

1-00 Lunch

2-15 The ABA rules

3-15 Discussion

3-45 Break

4-15 Basic Skills (practical)

5-30 Competition and the ABA medical scheme

6-15 Close

After a weekend like that I'll admit I didn't fancy going back, but I wasn't going through all that for nothing and I wanted that coaching badge. Two weeks later we were back for another weekend and it felt like we'd never been away.

PART TWO - SATURDAY

9-15 Course assembles

9-30 Basic Skills (practical)

10-45 Break

11-15 Seconding

12-15 Basic Skills (practical)

1-00 Lunch

2-15 Essentials of fitness

3-00 Fixed load circuit training (Theory/Practical)

3-45 Break

4-15 Basic Skills (practical)

5-30 Discussion

6-15 Close

PART TWO - SUNDAY

9-15 Course assembles

9-30 Basic Skills (practical)

10-45 Break

11-15 Organising a gym session for junior boxers

12-15 Running as a conditioner

1-00 Lunch

2-15 Basic Skills (practical)

3-15 Course revision

4-15 Basic skills assessment

5-00 ABA rules assessment

5-45 Discussion

6-15 Close

You see it is very time consuming and there is a lot of things involved but it wasn't that bad and a couple of weeks later Neil and I got our results and we both passed with flying colours. So now the Boys Welfare did have three qualified boxing coaches. I think the noble art of boxing should be on the school curriculum like it was many years ago. At least, the basics should be taught in my opinion.

Little did we know at the time but it was a unique year and we would have three boxers in the National ABA finals, a feat never done before in this town and never likely to be done again. An unbelievable achievement for a small club and we had four open class boxers. We also had a lad called Mo who was raw and needed schooling, but he was enthusiastic and a good trainer and reached the National novice final but got outpointed in the final.

Two lads fresh out of the Army came for a change of scenery, and boxed for the club, England International Kevin Bennett and Super-Heavyweight Billy Bessey. We also had ABA champions Ian Cooper and Michael Hunter who were also England Internationals. What a cracking little squad we had.

I became close friends with Kevin Bennett, I liked the way he was polite and had good manners. You go a long way when you have both and he did. There was an old saying that went 'It's nice to be important, but it's important to be nice', I really like that but it seems bad manners are the 'in thing' of today's youth and it's not nice at all, I don't like bad manners.

I took two junior boxers to the Royal Armouries in Leeds to box, there was another club in town going so we went in the same van and shared the petrol. Graham gave us a dodgy van to go in, by dodgy I mean the brakes were really bad and when I reached Timmy's house I jumped in the passenger seat and let him drive. Timmy would later have a World champion in Savannah Marshall. After a few hair raising moments we got there in one piece, all the lads boxed and we all managed to get home safe and sound but that van vas a death trap and wasn't road worthy.

The first fights Benny and Billy had for our club the show was a sell-out. Benny fought a Russian over four rounds, the Russian was over here boxing for a Sheffield club and had won twenty odd fights in a row. There certainly wasn't any cherry picking going on. After four brilliant rounds by two quality lads Benny won a close decision. Billy also won a close decision over Paul King, some years after this King got a life sentence for raping prostitutes at knife point and beating them up. Strange world we live in.

There was a big following everywhere the lads boxed, the town was bitten by the boxing bug that year and the local paper followed our adventures. It was a really good time and you could feel you were a part of something special.

We travelled the length and breadth of the country boxing. Glasgow, Edinburgh, Newcastle, Sunderland, Leeds, Sheffield, Liverpool, Manchester, Coventry, London and lots other places. We had some good nights in Scotland and were always invited back and some places would come outside and clap us off because they appreciated the quality of our boxers. They couldn't believe how one small club could go up there and beat the best boxers in Scotland. We were always given a warm welcome and some of them came down to watch the lads in the regional rounds of the ABAs.

We had five boxers entered in the ABA championships and three of them boxed the reigning National champion in the North East finals. Lightweight Mo Helel lost a very close decision that could have gone either way against the reigning champ. Graham almost pulled Mo out the week previous because he was fighting a real toe to toe merchant called Irum Greenwell, but he let him go and if he was taking too much he was going to throw the towel in but he shocked everyone by his gutsy display and beat Greenwell. Our Light-Welterweight Kevin Bennett had stopped a lad called Donkin in two rounds the week before and was in against the reigning champ Nigel Wright, the lad who beat him in the championships last year and got his spot on the Commonwealth Games team. There was a lot of needle in that fight but Benny fought like a tiger and got his revenge. Billy Bessey won and Michael Hunter went through. Our Middleweight Ian Cooper had a grudge match with the defending champ John Pearce, who had also won the Commonwealth Games Gold the previous year. They were 1-1 in the ABAs and both had won the National title but this was to be a win for Pearce in a quality fight. So after the excitement of the regional rounds and the North East finals (which some of the Middlesbrough football team attended) we had three boxers who progressed to the National quarter-finals. I can't recall who fought who in the quarter-finals at Coventry but we had three winners. I remember John Pearce lost a close decision to Carl Froch but Pearce was really boxing with one hand because he had hurt it badly in the win against Ian Cooper and almost pulled out. It's funny how things like that stick in your mind.

The semi-finals were held at the York Hall in Bethnal Green and after the weigh-ins there was plenty of time to kill so I went for a spot of lunch in the Blind Beggar. Then I went to Charlie Magri's sports shop, Charlie was a four time ABA champ in the 1970s and World Flyweight champ in 1983 as a pro. I had a chat with Charlie and we spoke about the Feeney brothers from Hartlepool and how he boxed both of them as an amateur and once when he boxed George Feeney in Hartlepool he and his coach were chased by a gang of Skinheads.

As fight time approached the place was packed out and everyone was buzzing. First up for us was Bantamweight Michael Hunter, he boxed brilliant and won a wide decision and he went in to his third consecutive ABA final, his other two were at Flyweight. Then Kevin Bennett at Light-Welterweight was fighting Jon Honney for a spot in the final. I've never seen Benny more fired up than he was for this fight, talk about eye of the tiger, he tore straight into Honney and tore him apart. The fight was over in 45 seconds and Honney had been down twice.

During the interval I was walking through the crowd and heard a voice say 'Alright' and it was Charlie Magri I couldn't believe he remembered me. He said "Michael Hunter won eh" and we talked for a short time.

Last up was our Super-Heavyweight Billy Bessey and he stopped a big feller from Swindon in the second round for a clean sweep. Our little club had three boxers in the National ABA finals.

The biggest day ever in Hartlepool's amateur boxing history was finally upon us and loads of fans and friends made their way to Barnsley Metrodome to support the lads. Ironically all our lads were up against Repton lads. Repton from London have been the biggest amateur boxing club in the country for many years.

We got off to a good start when Michael Hunter just scraped home to win the title at Bantamweight in a great little battle. He came on strong in the last round to nick it 10-9. It was four rounds then and the controversial computer scoring system.

Next up was Kevin Bennett and what happened here made me realise how corrupt the amateur officials were, they all should have been banned for life but they are in each other's pockets so what can you do. Benny punched his opponent from pillow to post and I thought the fight was going to be stopped at one stage as the other lad was taking a beating. The fight wasn't even close, Benny won it by a landslide but when they announced he'd lost 9-8 everyone was gobsmacked. The worst decision I've ever seen. Benny won that fight and should have won that title we were all gutted for him.

The last fight of the night was the big men and saw the last Hartlepool v Repton encounter. Billy Bessey v Joe Young, which turned out to be a thriller and the crowd went wild. When the bell ended the second round Young hit Billy twice and should have been disqualified as Billy wobbled back to his corner doing a funny walk. All looked lost and I think he might have stayed on his stool if Graham didn't say to him "Go out and win it the proper way". Billy's nose was bust and there was blood all over his face and he had taken a couple of counts, Young was going in to finish him off when Billy pulled out a huge right hand that landed flush and Young went down and was counted out to spark delirious scenes. Billy said it was the best punch he'd ever thrown and also said "It was the best moment in my life". The first few fights Billy had for our club he wore a white vest that looked like it had just came off the back of Harold Steptoe. He said he needed a new vest and I had a green Nike one that I gave him and jokingly told him if he inherits a bit of my power he'll go undefeated. All joking aside he won 13 fights in a row including the ABA title so a bit of the Horsley magic did rub off on him.

LAST STAND

Kevin Bennett had done all he could in the amateur game and had a brilliant career and was now ready to shed the vest and turn pro but the England squad named him in the upcoming Multi Nations so he boxed for his country and came away with a bronze medal. Then he turned pro.

Ian Cooper also hung up his amateur vest and joined his club mate Benny on the pro circuit. Neil Fannan took out a trainer's license and I got my seconds license. I had to go to a meeting of the Northern Area Council of the British Boxing Board of Control and answer questions put to me by the members. Dave Garside, a former British Heavyweight title challenger spoke up for me, and I had to wait outside for five minutes until I was told my application was successful.

The local paper came out and done a story about 'The New Gym' and there was a picture of Fannan, Cooper, Bennett and myself. The lads had their pro debuts at the Tall Trees in Yarm and it was full to the brim. We were relaxing in the hotel before the show and The Nutty Professor was on the TV. We were crying with laughter at it. Neil hadn't seen it before and he was laughing that much he started slavering which made us laugh even more. An ex-pro who was with us started to get changed into his tracksuit and when he took his trousers off, his vest was tucked in his underpants and everyone looked at each other and couldn't breathe. I swear to god we were crying. It was the funniest night ever before a boxing show. We still talk about it today. All that laughter stopped any pre-fight tension and both Benny and Cooper won their debuts impressively.

Dave Garside promoted some fantastic Sunday afternoon shows at the Mayfair Centre in Hartlepool, every show was sold out and those shows had some outstanding fights on. Michael Hunter turned pro and joined the stable and was in some exciting fights on the shows, some of the shows had some awesome guests like Brian London and Ernie Shavers, Great days.

I worked the shows for almost two years, Kevin Bennett went 9-1 in that time, but I never renewed my license because a guy from South Wales called Julian Davies interviewed me for an upcoming book called Streetfighters and the local paper ran a story about it, and if I renewed my license I would have to answer questions about my Street fighting days. I didn't think it was any business of theirs and that was the reason I didn't renew it.

Just after Benny turned pro we went down the country to do a bit of work, it was all outside work and it was bitterly cold. There were four or five of us in a flat and when we went back after work, Benny went out for a run, he wasn't happy going out in that weather but he was a professional boxer and had to keep his fitness up, anyway he got lost which pissed him off and it took him a while to find the flat. He thought a nice hot bath before he got his tea would sort him right out but when he ran the bath there was no hot water as it had all been ran off, so 'fuming' he had a cold 'bird bath'. Refreshed but in a bad mood he went to get his food out the fridge and it wasn't there? All that was in the fridge was a scabby little jacket potato and a knob of butter. He looked at my plate and said "Richy you are eating my fuckin' scran", I looked down at my plate, then looked at him, then looked at the scabby tatie in the fridge as he held the door open and said, "Oh no, you know what I might have done, picked yours up by mistake". They always say a hungry fighter is the best fighter it keeps the fire in their belly. Benny didn't believe me for some reason but we all make mistakes, sorry mate.

Then my sister Jackie killed herself age 38. It was hard to believe she would do anything like that as she had six children. I still can't get my head around it that she would commit suicide and leave her kids, she absolutely worshipped them and I find it hard to believe. On the day of her funeral I had some time alone with her and if you had a picture of sleeping beauty in your mind it would be my sister in her coffin. When our Debra and I went to the Hospital morgue to identify our Jackie, Kevin Bennett and his wife Gemma were in the same hospital at the same time and Gemma gave birth to their daughter Keeley. One left the earth and another came in. I never forgot the coincidence of it.

A couple of years after my sister died my lovely mam Brenda gained her angel wings. I was sat talking to her and her eyes rolled and then she started to jerk, I was in shock. I didn't know she was having a heart attack. She died in front of me and I was in complete shock, here one minute and gone the next. It done my head in and I coped by going out drinking to numb the pain. I was getting wasted all the time down the town, I was still working on the cables but my mind wasn't on the job so I did the right thing and packed it in, I needed to get myself in order first. I was knocking people out down the town because I was hurting. One night I was in the night club and an ex-boxer came over to me and started being all aggressive shouting shit like "I don't give a fuck about anyone me" and crap like that. I was thinking 'what are you talking about' and he was in my face again, then the penny dropped and I looked around and I saw everyone was looking over and I knew he must have said to them 'watch me offer him outside', so I told him to go away before I chinned him and he went back over to his mates. God knows what he said to them because within a minute he was back over in my face being an arsehole. I had already warned him so he wasn't getting another. I put my pint down and put a right hand through his head and he went down like a sack of shit, he was in spasm on the floor and I remember thinking 'That's my finish with coming down the town and all dickheads that come with it. If I don't stop coming down here I'll end up in prison because of one of these wankers', and I've kept to my word and never been down since. It's not worth it. I would rather have a few whiskies at home watching TV. That's my idea of a good chill out night.

I had agreed to an unlicensed fight in London with an 81 fight big-hitter called Gary Marcel. I hadn't been in the gym for a while and was unfit and overweight but there was another thing I had to add to the equation and it was a big factor, I was also 40 years old. I wasn't a fit 40 I was a fat 40. I didn't have the motivation to go to the gym and get in shape, and to tell the truth, my heart wasn't in it anymore. The last time I had a pair of boxing gloves on was when I knocked out Tony Louis in 90 seconds, but as the fight day drew closer I was in the mind set of "I'll go out and throw bombs in the first round and it'll be over".

I didn't know that a dark cloud was hanging over my head, in the shape of a very bad head cold, and could only breathe through my mouth. Three days before the fight I came down with a banging head and runny nose and by fight night I was as bad as a dog and was in no fit state to fight as it had travelled through my body and I was weak as piss. I should have done the right thing and pulled out but I had travelled to London so why come all this way and not fight, even if I was in such bad shape. I spoke with Benny who was working my corner and he knew how bad I was, he advised me to pull out. I had an argument on the phone with the promoter, I can't recall what it was about -maybe I was feeling sorry for myself and told him I might pull out- but when he phoned me about an hour later I answered the phone by shouting "fuckin' what" and not surprisingly he put the phone down on me. I had never pulled out of a fight in my life and wasn't going to on my last one. I decided before I came down here that this would be my last one whatever happened. I said to Benny "let's get ready for a fight" and he laughed and we got our gear together and headed to the venue.

When I got in the ring and started to trade punches with Marcel I was weak as a kitten and had no power in my punches and it dawned on me I was in for a hard night. Some people would have taken the easy way out and went down and stayed down to save themselves further punishment, but not me.

Marcel hit me with bomb after bomb and tried his hardest to knock me out but I was in survival mode because I had nothing in the tank and had no artillery to hurt him with and keep him at bay, so I used all my years of experience to get me through. In the third round he almost took my head off and I took a knee to get a breather. I was taking big gulps of air through my mouth because I couldn't breathe through my nose with the heavy head cold. He was all over me trying to finish me so I spat my Gum shield out to get a few vital seconds. The onslaught came again and I was on the ropes taking some big shots to the head, then I got a little spurt of adrenaline from somewhere and started trading with him. I fought my way off the ropes and turned him and let a six punch combination go. The roof almost came off as the two thousand spectators were all roaring and screaming at the tops of their voices. There was no power in my shots they were mainly arm punches and when I went to step in with a shot when he was on the ropes, my legs were like lead and stayed rooted to the spot, so I just fell in to him. Afterwards Marcel said I rocked him badly with a left hook on the ropes. Imagine if I was fit and that shot landed with power behind it, goodnight Vienna. I took a lot of punishment but he couldn't knock me out even as poorly as I was.

I showed a lot of heart and grit when I was in the trenches and won a lot of fans by my heroic 'last stand'. The unlicensed boxing legend Roy Shaw was ringside and paid me a lovely compliment by saying "Richy Horsley is a modern day Gladiator".

A lot of people who write books about their lives make themselves out to be like supermen and say they have never lost a fight. Even though they have been knocked out, they don't put any of their defeats in, which in my opinion makes the book false. Tell it like it was, put it all in, put the defeats in, everyone gets beat. Me, I put them all in for people to read, it makes me human like everyone else. We are all flesh and blood.

That was me finished with the fight game or at least I thought it was. I didn't know that a few years later I would train a bare knuckle fighter to go to the top of the tree and what a journey that was. Hold on to your seats because I'm going to tell you about it very soon.

I was working at my pals place doing bits n bobs until the recession hit and after that I thought I'd do a little education so I went to College and passed some exams. Level 2 Maths, Level 3 English, Level 3 History, Level 3 Psychology. You know what I enjoyed it and wish I had done it sooner. I had plans of becoming a Probation Officer. I worked for them as a volunteer for about six months and while I was getting a little experience I was also applying for jobs that came up like looking after the people doing community work etc but I never was never successful with any of the interviews, I believe it was my past. They would have me working for them for nothing as a volunteer but not on the payroll. I would have been a good addition for them and I think I would have done a good job but I wasn't working for nothing, I needed to bring a wage in so I stopped doing it and went to work elsewhere.

I met Wendy in 2010 and we have been inseparable ever since and got married on Christmas Eve 2014. We both love Christmas so Christmas Eve seemed a good time for us, from jingle bells to wedding bells. We both work hard and enjoy our holidays abroad. She is my soul mate and I couldn't imagine life without her. Oh yeah and I'm back on the cables working as a cable puller.

THE BULLDOG

I had been out of the fight game for years when I was asked to be a judge at a bare knuckle title fight in Nottingham. It was BKB known as bare knuckle boxing and it was legal, as long as there were rules put in place and safety measures like a boxing ring, referee, judges, paramedics and ambulance on hand, fighters to be checked over by the doctor on the afternoon of the show and weighed, if they didn't pass the pre-fight medical then they didn't fight full stop. It was just like a boxing show without the boxing gloves, but the fighters wore a small bandage on their hands to give the hand a little protection. Also it wasn't a ten second count but a twenty second count.

I went down to Nottingham with my wife Wendy and my mate Tommy and watched the show and judged the title fight. I saw some old faces and met some new ones. It was my wife's first experience of it and she enjoyed it. You would be surprised how many women where there. I started getting invited to a lot of BKB shows to judge fights, some I did and some I didn't, and realised it was still in my blood although this time I was on the other side of the ropes and it was nice to be recognised by people who wanted their photo taken with me.

I spoke about the BKB shows to my good pal Kevin 'Bulldog' Bennett who was a Commonwealth champion as a professional boxer but had been retired for around a decade. He started coming to the shows with me and my wife and soon he got bit by the bug. The promoters said they would love to have Benny on their shows so we had a chat about it. Benny said he fancied a go but will take it one fight at a time and see how far we go. It could all be over after one fight as you can break your hand pretty easy in BKB and that's you out of action and at Benny's age we didn't have the time to have long spells of inactivity. Benny asked me to train him and I said yes. He said we'll start this journey together and finish it together, and so began our BKB journey.

The first fight was in Newcastle against a Geordie called John Spencer, a veteran of 200 fights. Benny trained hard and was ready for his BKB debut. After the weigh-in we went to an Italian restaurant and got some pasta down us, pasta is excellent carbs for energy and a great pre-fight meal. This became our ritual after every weigh-in. I asked him how he was feeling ahead of his BKB debut and he said he was nice and relaxed and was looking forward to the fight.

Lots of people from Hartlepool made the trip, even triple Super-Bantamweight champion Michael Hunter was there to roar his old mate on.

Benny made his entrance to Queen's We Will Rock You, which got the crowd singing and the atmosphere was red hot. At the opening bell Benny didn't mess around and went straight on the attack. He set the body shots up perfectly and they landed with sickening thuds. Spencer went down three times and was counted out in less than two minutes. He made a statement with that knockout, he was back and it was like he'd never been away.

A few months later Benny had his next BKB fight against another 200 fight veteran called Mally Richardson. Lots of fans made the trip down to Nottingham and left happy as Benny made short work of Richardson, dropping him three times and knocking him out in the first round.

Our BKB adventure was picking up speed because of Benny's quality and his boxing background and experience. He had fought at the top level as a boxer. His next fight was a title eliminator against the unbeaten Brad Harris.

A few days before the fight, Benny's beloved dog Hagler died. Benny and his family were devastated. They picked him out when he was a few days old and had him since he was six weeks and he had always been one of the family. Benny contemplated pulling out of the fight as his mind wasn't on the job, he was grieving for his dog and I wouldn't have blamed him if he did pull out but he decided to fight.

We went to Coventry and Benny wasn't his usual self, he didn't have to say anything to me I understood. I just tried to say the right things at the right time. After the weigh-in we went for our usual Italian and got fuelled up on pasta.

As the fight drew closer he got changed into his war clothes and I talked to him trying to get his mind in fight mode. He got warmed up and we were called to the ring. No going back now. When the bell rang Benny switched immediately into fight mode and fought his usual fight. Harris was tough but outgunned and Benny dropped him three times on the way to a unanimous decision. He had taken care of business.

The World title fight was set for August 13 in Nottingham, and would be over 5 rounds and if he won he would make history as the first ever amateur boxing champion, professional boxing champion and World bare knuckle boxing champion.

BKB (Bare Knuckle Boxing) has weight divisions of one stone, 9-10 stone, 10-11 stone, 11-12 stone, 12-13 stone, 13-14 stone, etc. Benny was in the 11-12 stone division known as Lightweight in the BKB world. The sanctioning body is the WBKBC (World Bare Knuckle Boxing Council).

Benny's opponent was a hard-as-nails Welshman called Sean George, who was a come forward slugger with a big heart and had a kick boxing background where he won a British title. Sean won his eliminator by knock out.

Ironically Benny and Sean were on the same bill when Benny had his debut and both won impressively. They were both in the same weight division so we knew it was inevitable they would fight one day.

We had a good training camp and also done some training on the beach, he was fit and raring to go. The interest was immense and Benny sold loads of tickets. We had a good old sing song in the car on the way to Nottingham listening to Elvis.

At the weigh-in when they faced off, one of the Welsh supporters shouted 'Easy work Sean, Easy work', that was the wrong thing to say as it pissed Benny off. After the weigh-in we went for our usual Italian.

The atmosphere in the Colwick Hall Hotel was unbelievable and both sets of supporters were in great voice.

Benny went straight on the attack and put Sean on the back foot, he was all business. In the second round Benny hit Sean with a peach of a shot under the eye and it started to swell immediately. After three rounds of intense fighting Sean's eye was completely closed and his corner wanted to pull him out but he said no. The two fighters put on a breath taking five rounds of blood and guts action. The fight had everything apart from a knockdown. It was rated as the best BKB fight ever seen in a ring. Benny won a unanimous decision and became World champion. Sean went to Hospital and was told he had a broken nose and broken eye socket. Benny and Sean became good friends after that epic fight.

Well who would have thought when we set out on our bare knuckle boxing journey it would take us to the World title, it doesn't come better than that. The stuff dreams are made of.

We spoke about what he wanted to do next. Retire? He said he wanted to make the belt his own so wanted three more fights and then call it a day.

His first defence was on Bonfire night in Gateshead against an old opponent Brad Harris, after the original opponent pulled out. Brad had fought Benny six months previous and fancied his chances this time. Benny had added the Bulldog title to his name by now. He was known as the Bulldog as a pro so kept the name.

Before we set off on the journey to Gateshead we popped to see Nigel Benn who was in Hartlepool that day and we had a picture taken and he wished Benny good luck with the fight.

After the weigh-in we went to the Metro Centre and found an Italian's and loaded up on carbs, pasta all the way. Then Benny went for a lay down for a couple of hours.

In the venue there was a balcony so we went for a look while the action was playing out in the ring and when Benny's supports spotted him on the balcony they were all singing "There's only one Kevin Bennett", it was brilliant.

Brad was boxing well and was competitive in the first round until Benny dropped him with an overhand right.

He had a go in the second round and cut Benny over the eye but Benny was on his game and stepped up the pressure and was relentless. The referee stopped the fight in the third round after Harris paid numerous visits to the canvas.

INJUSTICE AND REDEMPTION

Benny made a quick second title defence a week before Christmas in Hartlepool and it was the first time ever such an event had been held in the town. As you can imagine it sold out straight away and hundreds of fans who had followed Benny around the country wanted to see the champ defend the title in his hometown.

A few hours before the show was due to start, the council turned up and told the promoters that if they use 'The Domes', nobody can take any alcohol in because it hasn't got a drinks license so the show would be cancelled. I wonder why they done that at the last minute instead of saying it weeks before when it was all arranged. So at the 11th hour the show was moved over the road to a site used for crazy golf of all things. It was totally unsuitable and there was no heating and it was like being in Siberia but at least the show was saved, although it was a shambles from the beginning to the end.

Benny's challenger was Conor McGregor's former sparring partner Liam James, who was a very tough and solid pressure fighter. Liam had loads of MMA fights and had trained for 12 months with Conor McGregor and became close friends with the MMA legend. He'd had some bare knuckle fights and fought his way into contention. We knew it was a dangerous fight but we didn't think Liam posed too much of a problem. The only problem we thought we might have would be his lack of respect for the rules, because he came from MMA and in the heat of battle he could resort back to it. Although there was a referee so he would surely keep check of anything underhand if it were to happen.

After the weigh-in we went for our usual plate of pasta and then chilled out until the fight drew near. The place was packed with

Benny's fans and family and my wife and her friends. Benny's son Jake carried the championship belt into the ring and we were ready to go.

After the opening bell our worst thoughts became reality when Liam grabbed Benny behind the neck and pulled his head down onto his fist and punched him rapidly four times in the face. This was an illegal move in boxing rules and BKB is under boxing rules. The referee didn't say a word, he should have at least stopped the action and gave him a warning and took a point off but he didn't do anything he let it continue. Liam then grabbed Benny around the neck and threw him off balance and there was still no warning off the ref, while off balance and trying to steady himself, Benny catches a punch and goes to the ropes. Finally the referee calls a halt to it and gives the T sign and shouts 'TIME' loud and clear, the first round was only twenty seconds old. When a referee calls 'time' the timekeeper automatically stops the clock. Liam goes to a neutral corner and the doctor is called to look at Benny's cut which looks like a bad one. The doctor told me he couldn't let Benny continue because the cut is so deep you can see the skull and he showed me. Benny was devastated because he wanted to continue, he hadn't landed a punch in the twenty seconds the fight lasted. The doctor told the ref that he had to stop the fight and he waved it off and Liam was announced as the new champion. Everyone was in shock. Surely it was a no contest. No said the promoters, Liam won fair and square. There's nothing fair about fighting dirty. It's not in the boxing rules that you can fight dirty and not get disqualified. The twenty seconds the fight lasted Liam fought dirty and nothing was done about it. What a farce. The promoters UBBAD went down in a few people's estimation the way they refused to deal with it. The aftermath was a war of words on social media between fans of the two fighters. I wanted answers and the WBKBC who sanctioned the fight, wouldn't even give me a reply to any of my questions they just chose to ignore me. They knew they had made a mistake but didn't want to admit it. It was inexperience on their part as far as I was concerned. They were hoping it would go away but they weren't going to brush this under the carpet. UBBAD promotions kept quiet about it and the arguments on social media about the injustice of them taking an undefeated champion's title away like that was shocking and they can't do it under boxing rules. I couldn't stop thinking about it and it spoiled my Christmas. I would wake up in the middle of the night thinking about it and not be able to get back to sleep. It really did my head in.

About six months previous to this they brought a rule out that hand wraps were banned and you could only use a certain type of bandage that was supplied by the WBKBC and signed off by their representative. Liam had worn banned hand wraps against Benny. How was he allowed to do that? I was told that Liam had bandages on and got them signed off, then took them off and put the banned had wraps on. Surely he would be disqualified after a hearing? No hearing and still no reply to any of my questions.

The arguments were going on every day on social media. Some said Liam won fairly because it was a punch that caused the cut, but most said Benny should be given the title back and the fight called a no contest. The cut was caused by an illegal punch through dirty tactics using illegal bandages. It was a no brainer what the result should be. Pulling a man's head down and punching it four times and then grabbing him round the neck and throwing him have no place in a boxing ring under boxing rules. That's why Liam should have been warned or disqualified but neither happened, therefore the fight should have been declared a no contest but that didn't happen either. Imagine if a proper boxing referee was in the ring that night, what would the result have been? What an absolute cock up the WBKBC made of the whole situation and I lost all respect for them by the way they chose not to deal with it. All they did was announce an immediate rematch but Benny had to heal first because the cut on his forehead looked like he'd been hit by a sharp point, that's why it went deep and to the skull. I've never known a fist with a hand wrap on cause damage like that in all my years involved in the fight game.

The rematch was set for four months later in April at Coventry's Sky Dome, it wasn't a new place to us because Benny fought there as a pro and won in two rounds. Luckily Benny's cut had healed by then and he kept ticking over with a bit of gym training and a few runs before we went into a full six weeks training camp. The pain you couldn't see was the pain we felt inside, this was time to get even. The camp started off to a good omen because Benny was working local and so was I.

I trained Benny in the gym three times a week and we also brought in Steven Smith, a strength and condition coach and no stone was left unturned in our preparation. Once a week we headed off to another gym for quality sparring with one of the best amateur's in the country. After six weeks of blood, sweat and sacrifice Benny was primed and ready.

I had been putting training video snippets on social media each week because I know Liam would be watching them. Then one week he made a comment on his page about how he was sick of seeing these training videos and nothing will prepare the man who stands in front of him and crap like that. I knew then it was getting in Liam's head. It's all psychology. A week later when Liam was being interviewed about the upcoming fight, he exploded with a torrent of abuse what was aimed at me. All the stuff I'd been saying about their last fight calling Liam a cheat and a dirty fighter and a fake champion as well as other things, all came out of Liam's mouth and he was going to show everyone why they call him 'Bad Intentions'. I watched the interview a few times and couldn't stop laughing because I knew I had him. I was getting into his head.

For a full week before the fight Benny didn't go on social media at all, he kept his mind clear and focused on the fight. There were hundreds of people arguing about the last fight and who was going to win this one. It had been going on for four months. Benny's old buddy Billy Bessey had a £500 bet with one of Liam's fans.

The day before the fight I put a post on my page about Liam, so it would have the maximum effect and it added even more to the rivalry and hostility on both sides. I put the post on as a reply to Liam's outburst in his interview and chose the day before the fight as the perfect time, so it would be fresh in his mind and make him even lose a bit of sleep. Here is the post I put on.

LIAM JAMES – FAKE CHAMP

I would like to say a few words in reply to Liam James dissing me on social media. I don't like slagging fighters off because everyone who has the bottle to step through the ropes is a warrior in my eyes. Fighters are supposed to be gentlemen with morals, and respectful to others and set a good example. Liam James on the other hand is not respectful to others, is very arrogant and does not set a good example. He is a very over-rated BKB fighter and a dirty fighter. Whatever happened to 'Let's have a good clean fight', and then I addressed Liam directly and said

"Liam why do you fight dirty?"

"Is it because you know you will lose if you fight fair?"

"Is Liam James the most over-rated fighter in BKB today?"

I can hear you shouting at your phones and laptops and iPads, 'Yes'.

I had done my psychology on Liam.

I had many talks with Benny in the build-up. One talk was when I told him Skill, Brains and Guts will win this fight. The first thing is you have the skills to win this so use your skill. Secondly you don't just go in and fight you use your brains, move around, create openings, feint, counter, use your brains. Third, you need to have the guts to carry it out. If it goes into the trenches you've got to have the stomach for it. You've got to want it more. You've got to have the guts. A few times in training I'd remind him "Remember, Skill, Brains and Guts will win this fight".

Another discussion was how the fight itself would go. We knew Liam would come out from the opening bell like a tornado and would only have two good rounds in him at that pace, so we worked on boxing on the back foot for the first two rounds and weather the storm through Skill, Brains and Guts. Then after two rounds we knew the storm would have blown itself out. Then from the third round Benny would go to work and start sinking in the rib crippling body shots he's known for. We both said that Liam would do one of two things ...

1. Take his medicine and go down fighting

or

2. Quit

We would soon find out.

The journey to Coventry was a good one, I was confident we were going to right the wrong.

Liam arrived an hour late for the weigh-in because his lift let him down at the last minute. Apparently the guy's dog had died during the night but he didn't tell Liam until he was sat waiting for his lift. Talk about deserting a sinking ship. By the time Liam arrived to get weighed we were tucking into our usual pasta dishes.

The fights got under way and there were some beauties but the one they had come to see was the rematch between Bennett and James. You could feel it in the air, the anticipation on everyone was something else and the atmosphere was building. We had a walk about and spoke to the fans and family and others wishing Benny the best of luck before we went back and got the bandages on and got into fight mode. When the long awaited rematch was the next fight on, I bet some felt like they'd just woke up on Christmas morning.

There were lots of people screaming good luck to Benny over the music as we made our way to the ring. When Liam climbed through the ropes it was the first time I'd seen him since all the social media hostilities and we both glared at each other.

Just before the bell I was in Benny's ear telling him, "This is it, this fight will define your BKB career. This is how you'll be remembered. You need to put this right, it's now or never, remember skill, brains and guts".

The bell went and as expected Liam came charging out like a whirlwind and it was nothing but intense pressure. This is what we prepared for so Benny kept tucked up and boxed off the back foot, slipped, rolled and countered. At the end of the round I told him he was boxing lovely and keep to plan. "Keep slipping and countering and keep tucked up. He'll blow himself out in another round he can't keep this pace up"

Round two was a carbon copy of the first. About twenty seconds from the bell I knew Liam had shot his bolt and the hurricane was becoming a gentle breeze. I saw a little wobble on his legs as he walked back to his corner.

Benny had a small cut over and under his eye so as I was working on them I said "He is finished Benny. He's got nothing left. His legs wobbled as he walked back to the corner. If he comes out for this round sink some body shots in and it will be all over."

Before the bell rang for the third round the referee was called over to Liam's corner, he wasn't coming out for the third round, the fight was over. Kevin Bennett was champ again. Everything we talked about in the build-up all came true. Would Liam take his medicine and go down fighting or quit. He chose the latter.

Four months of pain and heartache was washed away in a single moment. What a satisfying win that was. Liam congratulated Benny and came over to me and shook my hand and I said to him "I don't hate you Liam. It was psychology to get in your head", "I know that now" he said.

When Kevin Bennett was announced as World champion again and the belt put round his waist, what an amazing feeling that was. A sense of achievement and a destiny fulfilled. A wrong had been corrected and we came out on top in the end. Justice was served.

We had said whatever the outcome this would be Benny's last fight and six days after regaining the title he announced his retirement from BKB. We both put out statements and here is mine for you to read.

"When we set out on this bare knuckle journey we had a goal in mind and that was to win the World 12 stone title. We achieved that goal. We brought, excitement, class, entertainment, and we put bums on seats.

We made memories, not only for ourselves and our families, but for the people who followed us.

When we started we said 'we'll start it together and finish it together' and that's exactly what we did.

We have both now retired from BKB as champions, with our respect and dignity intact and our heads held high."

We were overwhelmed with the well wishes from hundreds of people. Everyone was full of praise for what we done in the BKB world and it was nice to be thought of in such a way.

Benny's fight with Sean George was voted as the best BKB fight ever seen in a boxing ring and in another poll just before Christmas 2017, Benny was voted as the best British pound for pound BKB fighter ever.

Mission accomplished. We can move on with our lives now.

Hope you enjoyed the book.

Best Wishes

Richy Horsley

'30 YEARS A FIGHTER'

The Fighting Memoirs of KEVIN 'BULLDOG' BENNETT

with Richy Horsley

ISBN: 978-1-912543-09-0

30 Years A Fighter is the story of a unique fighter, Kevin 'Bulldog' Bennett. The book is currently being written with Richy Horsley.

Benny as he is known, was an amateur boxing champion. A professional boxing champion and a world bare knuckle boxing champion. How many people do you know have achieved that accolade? Nobody, only Kevin Bennett he is the first one.

He had his first fight at age 11 and his last fight at age 41, hence the title '30 Years a Fighter.'

Also available from Warcry Press

Battling Bowes

with Richy Horsley

ISBN: 978-1-912543-09-0

Battling Bowes is the story of the professional boxing career of George Bowes, the terror of the bantamweight and the featherweight divisions in the 1950s and 60s. He was a sporting hero in the North East with a large following. Working as a coal-filler in the Durham mines, the pale-faced pitman had such a devastating punch that most of the champions of the day tried to avoid him. He knocked out the European champion inside two rounds and the British champion in the first round. Both were non-title fights and both champions refused to put their titles on the line against Bowes. He was such an exciting fighter that his appearance on a boxing show usually meant it was a sell-out. The promoters loved him. His only handicap was he cut easily. There were usually fifty shades of claret at a Bowes fight. Boxing fans will enjoy this action packed story of one of boxing's forgotten heroes.

Coming soon from Warcry Press

Lee Duffy

'The Whole of The Moon'

by Jamie Boyle

ISBN: 978-1-912543-07-6

A book which has taken over 25 years to arrive. The definitive story of the man who held an eight-year reign of terror over the town of Boro. Containing many first hand and previously unheard accounts from some of Duffy's closest friends and associates, this book will finally confirm who the man was and what he was really all about. No stone will be left unturned and this book will not shy away from controversy but will aim to provide an unbiased and balanced view on the 'Borough icon. Make no mistake, this will be the definitive book on Lee Duffy, there will be no more 'ifs' and 'buts after its release. From the author of the bestselling Paul Sykes books 'Unfinished Agony' and 'Further Agony' Jamie Boyle.